The
Devil's
DP
Dictionary

The Devil's DP Dictionary

by

Stan Kelly-Bootle

McGraw-Hill Book Company

New York   St. Louis   San Francisco
Auckland   Bogotá   Hamburg   Johannesburg
London   Madrid   Mexico   Montreal
New Delhi   Panama   Paris   São Paulo
Singapore   Sydney   Tokyo   Toronto

Library of Congress Cataloging in Publication Data

Kelly-Bootle, Stan.
  The devil's DP dictionary.

  1. Electronic data processing—Dictionaries.
2. Electronic data processing—Anecdotes, facetiae,
satire, etc. I. Title.
QA76.15.K44   001.64'03'21   81–1053
                            AACR2

ISBN 0-07-034022-6

1 2 3 4 5 6 7 8 9 0 MUMU 8 9 8 7 6 5 4 3 2 1

The editors for this book were Barry Richman and Olive Collen, the designer was
Elliot Epstein, and the production supervisor was Sally Fliess. It was set in Compano
by ComCom.

Printed and bound by The Murray Printing Company.

To Iwonka, my inspirer and correctrice, whose pruf redding was feydeauesque but fun.

Acknowledgments

I have been exposed to computing (and vice versa) since 1953, and it would not be easy to list all those who have, knowingly or innocently, influenced the entries and diatribes in my dictionary. With numbing magnanimity I have acknowledged many known and suspected sources in the ensuing text, but the data processing whirligig has generated such a rich and volatile folklore that some errors and omissions must be expected. I invite proofs of violent injustices, so that future editions might dilute my claims to originality and reduce my exposure to litigation.

Entries marked [from JARGON FILE] are reproduced, with permission and minor changes, from a computerized glossary maintained at SAIL and MIT by Mark Crispin, Raphael Finkel, Guy L. Steele, Jr., and Donald Woods, with the assistance of colleagues from other AI communities. I am grateful to Prof. D. E. Knuth, Stanford University, for directing me toward this delightful source of DP wordage.

At odd moments during my compilation I have been helped by, and wish to thank, Dr. M. D. Godfrey, Dr. Wesley Walton, Mrs. Joan Smith, Chris Hipwell, Jim Joyce, Bob Toxen, Ernest Harpe, and Dr. D. F. Hartley.

I am greatly indebted to Peter Davies for guiding me through the maze of proper lexicographical usages, and to Peggy Lamb and Olive Collen for advice on American literary conventions and similar solecisms. Finally, which brings me to the top of my STACK (q.v.), I want to thank Barry Richman, my editorial mentor at McGraw-Hill, whose constant encouragement seldom failed to include an essential element of irksome cajolery.

Permission to quote, adapt, or parody material from the following sources is gratefully acknowledged.

abacus   Cartoon by Michele Coxon.

algorithm   Parody based on Ira Gershwin (lyrics) and George Gershwin (music), "I Got Rhythm," Chappell Music Company, New York.

console and **nest**   Parodies based on Richard Rodgers and Oscar Hammerstein II, "My Favorite Things," Williamson Music Inc., Chappell Music Company, New York.

decade counter   From H. Lukoff, *From Dits to Bits,* Robotics Press, Portland, 1979.

hexadecimal   From William Barden, Jr., *TRS-80 Assembly Language Programming,* Radio Shack Publications, 1979.

Jargon file   See entry.

lemma three   Parody based on Will Holt, "The Lemon Tree," Dolfi Music Inc., Chappell Music Company, New York.

numerology   From D. E. Knuth, *The Art of Computer Programming: Fundamental Algorithms,* vol. 1, Addison-Wesley, Reading, Mass., 1979.

Ogam   From *America BC,* by Barry Fell. © 1970 Quadrangle Books. Reprinted by permission of Times Books, a division of Quadrangle—The New York Times Book Company.

reality   Parody based on Betty Comden, Jule Styne, Adolph Green, "The Party's Over," Chappell Music Company, New York.

Introduction

This book is aimed at the dearth of useful data processing glossaries. It may well increase this dearth, but nevertheless I hope that it casts an amusing glare on the many linguistiç opacities which bedevil the computing trade. Ambrose Bierce (1842–1914?), the underappreciated inventor of cynical lexicography, defined the dictionary as "a malevolent device for cramping the growth of a language and making it hard and inelastic."[1] Whether we like it or not, language has never paid the slightest attention to such crampage—not once since that almighty cock-up at Babel (Genesis 11:1–9)—nor to the countless Académie-type crusades mounted to enforce goodspeak and proper usage. Indeed, the dictionary has recently been blamed for endorsing "shanty-town constructions" and lending authority to "how a sufficiently large number of half-literate immigrants talk."[2]

The computer revolution is still "too much with us" to justify a dogmatic "naming of parts"—or even a positive taxonomical posture —but we can learn from similar crises in the history of science. Linnaeus (1735) and Lavoisier (1787), for example, were faced with the problem of assigning new names to new and old objects (organisms and chemicals, respectively); their choice of "neutral" roots from the "dead" Latin and Greek established a trend followed by most scientific disciplines. The precision of the new appellations compared with the vernacular (e.g., not all cats are *Felis domesticus,* and there are salts other than sodium chloride) has had the negative side effect of alienating the nonscientist.

---

[1]Bierce's aphorisms, masquerading as definitions, first appeared in various California newspaper and magazine columns between 1881 and 1906. They were collated and issued "in covers" as the *Cynic's Word Book* (1906). A more complete edition emerged in 1911 as *The Devil's Dictionary* (Neale Publishing Company, New York). Bierce avoided the horrors of a conventional demise by disappearing in Mexico during the 1913–14 revolution.

[2]Lancelot Hogben, *The Vocabulary of Science,* Heinemann, London, 1969.

Introduction

The DP vocabulary is still very much based on Anglo-Saxon roots, reflecting the informality of the English/American pioneers, and underlining the fact that computer science is not yet ready for Linnaean classifications.

In the meantime, we survive merrily with our anthropomorphic *memory*, our medical *bug*, our sexual *random access*, our homely *address*, our gastronomic *chip*, our sportive *jump*, our ornithological *nest*, our narcotic *hash*, our thespian *mask*, our law's *delay*, our daily *queue*, and our slum's *degradation*.

Stan Kelly-Bootle
San Francisco, California, and Bargemon, Provence

Guide

Main entries, arranged in alphabetical order, are set in boldface type.

The meaning of an entry should always be ascertained *before* consulting this dictionary.

Parts of speech are shown in italics: *n.* (noun); *v.* (verb); *v. intrans.* (intransitive verb); *v. trans.* (transitive verb); *adj.* (adjective); *adv.* (adverb).

Pronunciations are indicated, rarely, between reversed virgules: \glass titty\

Etymologies are suggested between squarish brackets: [From Latin *aboriri* "to miscarry."]

Cross-references (implicit and explicit) are signaled by the typographical nuance of small-capital letters.

Diatribes following the so-called definition are offset in a minuscule font—beyond the reach of legal beagality.

The
Devil's
DP
Dictionary

abacus *n*. [From Latin *abacus* "a back up."] A reliable solid-state biquinary computing device now partly superseded by the Cray series.

▶The venerable bead still has many champions, but most attempts to refine the technology have proved self-defeating, to say the least. The Irish Business Machines megabead frame with gravity-assisted multisliding, for example, failed to catch on, even in the lucrative Russian point-of-sale market. Some blame the excessive miniaturization adopted to provide 64 K beads per wire; others point to the bewildering array of color schemes used to distinguish mantissa and exponent in the various floating-bead sections. The original, time-honored abacus (see the illustration on page 2), which can be manipulated without tweezers and microscopes survives as a useful standby for systems such as the NCR500, the Spectrum I, and the IBM-1400. ISO Maintenance Bulletin 2, covering the monthly greasing of cross wires, should be strictly observed if maximum bead rates are required. For a comprehensive abacalian bibliography see Martin Gardner, *Mathematical Circus*, Alfred A. Knopf, New York, 1979.

abend *n*. [From German *guten Abend* "good evening."] A system ABORT deliberately induced (usually on Fridays) to allow the third-shift staff to leave early.

ABM *n*. [Arab Business Machines.] A shadowy consortium rumored to be poised for an IBM takeover bid in the mid-1960s.

▶Cynics have claimed that ABM was a Zionist plot intended to flood the Arab world with early versions of OS 360. Others believe it was a genuine Arab attempt to switch from oil to a more profitable enterprise. Yet others postulated that the Judeo-Christian exploitation of the ALGORITHM, an Islamic invention (patents pending since 825 A.D.), had gone a little too far without the proper dues. A rhymester of the period captured the excitement:

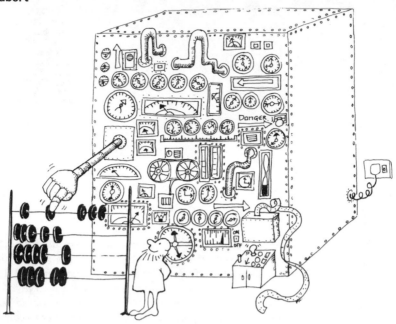

Haroun al-Raschid (may his revenues increase)
Awoke one night from a dream of peace;
He called his guards with eastern phlegm
And said, "Go buy me IBM!
Here's fifty billion, on the nail;
If there's any change, get me ICL!

A muezzin to call the compilers,
Mecca bureaus for service divine;
We'll remove the golf balls from the printers
And have eunuchs protecting each line."

abort *n. & v.trans.* [From Latin *aboriri* "to miscarry."] **1** *n.* The rather heavy interruption of a job or system, usually self-induced, but sometimes invoked by the user. *See also* ABEND. **2** *v.trans.* To terminate (a program, system, plan) in such a manner that future hopes and discussions of revivification attract predicates in the neighborhood of wishful. **3** *v.trans.* To conclude (a salesperson's visitation) by producing a loaded firearm of sufficient caliber.

ACATA *n.* [Acronym for the Association for Computer-Assisted Text Analysis.] An international organization working to establish an interuniversity network of machine-readable corpora. This will, for example, allow scholars in Canterbury to access the Chaucerian database at the University of California, Berkeley, while researchers in St. Louis are online to the T. S. Eliot disk at the Oxford University computer center.

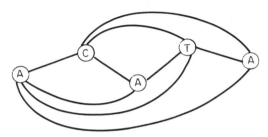

A rare example of acronymic graph theory.

ack *n.* [Origin: back-formed negation of NACK.] A signal indicating that the error-detection circuits have failed.

acronym *n.* [Acronym for Alphabetic Collocation Reducing Or Numbing Your Memory.] A memorable word from which a non-memorable phrase is acrostically generated; a circumlocutory abbreviation often confused with its antonym, MNEMONIC.

▶Devising an acronym is the first step in systems design. Contrary to common belief, acronyms are created by mapping initial letters onto words rather than the reverse. The former mapping is 1–many and therefore easier. This also explains the antimnemonicity of most acronyms. Many design teams manage without a resident full-time acronymist. This is fatal penny-pinching and explains the current low standards in DP acronymity. *See* the table on pages 4 and 5.

acuracy *n.* An absense of erors. "The computer offers both speed and acuracy, but the greatest of these is acuracy."—Anon. doctoral thesis on automation, 1980.

aerosol spray *n.* A container holding a pressurized panacea which can be released in a series of unskilled squirts. *Compare* Pandora; *see* the table on pages 6 to 8.

TABLE OF ACRONYMS

Acronym	Acrostic phrase	Owner, patentee, or acronymist
ALU	Arthritic-Logic Unit	Anon.
APL	A Packed Language	K. Iverson (ca. 1961)
ASCIII	American Standard Code for Interchanging Irrelevant Information	Anon.
AUGRATIN	Amalgamated Union of General Rewriters, Amenders, Tinkerers, & INterpolators	*See* PAYROLL
C	Computer	Irish Business Machines (1954) (*see* COMPUTER below)
CAD	Computer-Aided Delay	P. B. Fellgett (ca. 1973)
COMPUTER	Computer-Oriented Machine Performing Under The Electronic Regimen	Irish Business Machines (1954); dropped following complaints of undue recursion
DEBE	Does Everything But Eat	Supersoft Inc. (ca. 1980)
FUBAR	F***ed Up Beyond All Recognition	Worcester Polytechnic Institute (*see* JARGON FILE)
GIGO	Gospel In, Garbage Out	Anon.
ICARUS	Infallible, Comprehensive, And Running User Software	ICARUS Inc. (ca. 1979)
ICL	"I see hell"	International Computers Ltd.
IMP	Integrated Morticians' Package	ICARUS Inc. (more at IMP)

Acronym	Acrostic phrase	Owner, patentee, or acronymist
IRS	Internal Revision Service	*See* PAYROLL
ISAM	Intrinsically Slow Access Method	Anon.
JANUS	JANuary Updating Service	ICARUS Inc. *See* DECADE COUNTER
LINO	Last In, Never Out	Anon. (*See* STACK)
LISP	Lots of Irritating, Spurious Parentheses	J. McCarthy (ca. 1961)
MUM	MultiUse Mnemonics	S. Kelly-Bootle (1976)
MUNIFICENT	Most Unworthy Numerical Integrator Now Functioning In China; Evaluations Not Trustworthy	Kai Lung Computers Inc. (1950)
MUSE	Most Unusual Shakespearean Engine	W. Shakespeare (ca. 1582)
NEBULA	NEw BUsiness LAnguage	Ferranti Ltd. (ca. 1960)
OS	OutSized	Anon.
PTF	Permanent Temporary Fix	Anon.
SHIT	Square Holes In Tape	Considered but rejected by Olivetti (1958)
SNA	Scapegoat Network Architecture	Anon.
TOPE	Timesharing OPerators' Executive	*See* CURSOR
WOM	Write Only Memory	Anon.

TABLE OF ERROSOL INC.™ AEROSOL SPRAYS

Trade name	Function	Mode d'emploi
Smegma	Emits cheap, stale, personalized tobacco fumes, old coffee aromas, and the smell of busy peripherals	Before quitting prematurely, spray the computer room or data prep area for 30 seconds. Smegma persists for at least 8 hours, reassuring the next shift arrivals that they have just missed you
Writ-guard	Antilitigant. Repels 99% of all known attorneys, high court judges, monopolies, commissions, federal consumer protection agencies, *more*	Spray lightly and evenly over all writs, subpoenas, juries, DAs, exhibits, and sub-judice software. *Caution:* Avoid the innocent or guilty, whichever the case may be
Thesis	Imparts a scholarly gloss to your doctoral submission; adds donnish wit and waspish innuendo	Apply liberally to your ms and assessors. Double-spray the first and last pages and all footnotes and references
Compat	An effective general conversion aid. Gives instant compatibility with alien systems, both hardware and software. Used and recommended by *both* SHA members	Hold spray 3 inches from your *target* tape, card, compiler, DBMS, DPM, or CPU. Squirt and rotate to ensure an even covering of all bits, links, code holes, and subschemas. *Caution:* Do not spray the *source* environment!

Trade name	Function	Mode d'emploi
Walpurge	The sure-fire file and database purging and initiation remedy! Tried and tested with *all* media: ROM, PROM, EPROM (beats the most ultra UV!), core, mag'n'paper tape, hard'n'soft disks, paper'n'mag cards, bubbles, mercury delay lines, William's tubes, brunsvigas, *more*	Save *hours* cleaning those old files! One quick squelch nullifies all bit patterns (overflow areas, too!). For ivory abacus beads, a second application may be needed. *Caution:* Do not inhale! Your cellular DNA code may disappear
Launch	Ensures a smooth new model release. Impacts the market, *not* your old range!	Spray with abandon on your PR department, brochures, existing user base, and Press Day sandwiches
Shoo-bug	Instantly fixes all detectable BUGS! Soothes the undetectables! Ends your endless loops, supplies missing declarations, takes pounds off your flabby syntax while you sleep! Guaranteed effective, all languages, all levels! Why wait for that new compiler release? Save $$$$$ NOW! Prof. Knuth writes: "My secret is no more. Thanks to Shoo-bug, the era of the People's Algorithm has dawned."	Treat your suspect code before and after compilation. If the condition persists, treat the compiler. *Very* high-level languages may require repeated applications. Will not harm or stain error-free modules. Use only as directed

TABLE OF ERROSOL INC.[TM] **AEROSOL SPRAYS** (*continued*)

Trade name	Function	Mode d'emploi
New Improved Shoo-bug	*Incredibly,* the omnipotent, infallible Shoo-bug **plus** the added, secret metasyntactic element FOO!	Spray freely, as before. But *now* Shoo-bug works on your OS *and* on all documentation. *Caution:* Keep away from domestic animals and AI departments
Prop-Rite	Protects your software instantly. Prevents unauthorized copying of source or object code, whatever the medium	Apply sparingly to disks, tapes, and listings. Protection lasts 12 hours. Will not harm the most delicate programs
Steal	The essential spray for timeshare freaks and software thieves. Will break down the tightest security barriers. Converts all passwords to FOOBAR! and all files to public! Even overcomes Prop-Rite. Used by Control and Chaos agents the world over	For the best results, spray the target system. If this is not possible, spray the terminal and modem. Prop-Rited systems may need several applications to remove protection

aibohphobia *n.*   The fear of palindromes.

▶Sufferers who wish to succeed in the DP field should bend over backward to overcome this disability. It is not unknown for some stacks to pop in when they should have popped out, and vice versa. It is, therefore, sound programming strategy to ensure that *all* strings and sgnirts are made palindromic, and thereby immune from any trivial reversal-type transformations. A DP doctor writes: "Aibohphobia *can* be cured with a little cooperation from the patient. Those with mild attacks, characterized by a brief, passing irritation with palindromes, are usually taken through a gentle verbal therapy. I get them to repeat such phrases as 'Madam, I'm Fred,' 'Able was I ere I saw Josephine,' and 'A man, a plan, a canal, Suez!' In more severe cases, for example, with patients who shake uncontrollably at the sight of a radar, I often perform a rather pretty little hippocampectomy."

ALGOL 84 *n.* [Acronym for **ALGO**rithmic Language **84.**] An extension of ALGOL being formulated by 84 dissidents from various ALGOL user groups; every effort is being made to ensure that ALGOL 84 will be ready by 1984 and will not be a proper superset of ALGOL 68.

algorasm *n.* [Origin: blend of *algorism* + *orgasm.*] A sudden, short-lived moment of pleasure enjoyed by the programmer (and, for all we know, by the system) when the final KLUDGE rings the bell.

◗A DP psychiatrist writes: "However brief the thrill, and however many disillusions lie ahead, one's first algorasm is long remembered and savored. Many programmers, alas, in spite of years spent sweating over a hot terminal, have never attained this summit. Perhaps they try too hard. Learning to relax while the system recompiles your edited code is a good habit to acquire. And then one day, after a series of FLEEPs, when least expected, the magic 'No detected errors' message will fill your screen. In their classic, *The Algorasm Dissected: A Prolonged Study of Person-Machine Intercourse in the Climactic Environment,* Masters and Thumps have described a variety of algorasmic step functions, the many different tumescent plateaus possible before the final, massive tintinnabulation, or the 'real McCoy' as we psychiatrists prefer to call it. After the Holy Grail has come home to roost in the ballpark, expect a period of deflation, or perhaps even self-doubt and guilt.

"Some of my patients, disregarding the mural caveats, light up a cigarette and ask themselves, 'O God, do I really *deserve* so much happiness?' This is such a crazy attitude I could scream. Relish that moment, I say, feel good and comfortable, even though the algorasm may signal a project completed and the need to seek employment elsewhere! Fresh fields and postures new lie ahead. The frequency and intensity of your algorasms will certainly improve with a change of system, and who knows, maybe a coarser language and a less inhibited operating environment await you. A log of your previous climaxes with date, place, language, OS, etc., can spice the weakest résumé, but keep the narrative crisp and objective. Your prospective employer cannot be expected to wade through a forum of boastful confessionals: 'As I stroked the keyboard, I felt my patellae stiffening; *yes, yes* implored the screen, just one line more, escape . . .' and similar hyperbole are unlikely to impress a bank seeking some RPG fixes in the School Savings package. Simple entries such as '03/15/78:2.00A.M.; made it with VM/370; all the way; wow; three days to recover' are infinitely more effective.

9

"Patients often ask me what the *normal* algorasmic frequency is—a typically misguided attempt to quantify the unquantifiable. If you are content to write and run furtive FACTORIAL N routines in FORTRAN, a meaningless masturbatory exercise, there is, of course, no limit to your daily emission rate. Similarly, there are voyeurs and kibitzers who achieve dauntingly high climactical averages by invading someone else's interactive space. So there is, and I stress this regularly at $150 per stress, no conceivable pattern of algorasmic activity or inactivity that can be in any way characterized as *abnormal*. As DP involvement sinks downward into socioeconomic groups unaware of the cost-effectiveness of psychiatry, our profession and fee scales will maintain their traditional integrity. The humblest of personal computer owners will be treated no differently from our major mainframe victims."

algorism *n.* A pre-LISP ALGORITHM devised by abu-Ja'far Mohammed ibn-Mūsa al-Khuwārizmi (Persian mathematician fl. A.D. 825) who wrote the first BASIC substring modifier in a vain attempt to shorten his name.

▶There is much unexplored and spurious evidence that he cooperated with his poet-mathematician friend Omar Khayyâm in many other areas of anachronistic computer science. Alas, the demon drink then (as now) clearly interrupted the study of stacks and boolean algebra.

For 'IS' and 'IS-NOT' though with Rule and Line,
And 'UP-and-DOWN' by Logic I define,
Of all that one should care to fathom, I
Was never deep in anything but—Wine.

(Tetrasich #58, Rubâiyât; tr. E. FitzGerald.)

Omar's entire output reflects that poignant, calvinistic despair common to all computer scientists. Then (as now) progress was stultified by the lack of effective text-editing facilities:

The Moving Finger writes; and, having writ,
Moves on: Nor all your Piety nor Wit
Shall lure it back to cancel half a Line,
Nor all your Tears wash out a Word of it.

(Tetrasich #76. Op. cit.)

algorithm *n.* [Origin: ALGORISM with a pronounced LISP.] A rare species endangered by the industry's cavalier pursuit and gauche attempts at domestication.

▶The current plight of the unspotted algorithm, *Algorithmus accuratus,* can be traced back to overculling in the 1960s. It will be recalled that the previous decade had witnessed an uncontrolled population growth, indeed a plague of the creatures in diverse academic terrains. Their pernicious invasion of the commercial environment in the late 1950s prompted IBM to offer the controversial $4.98 bounty per pelt. Hordes of greedy and unskilled people from all walks of life deserted their jobs and families, sold their possessions, and flocked to dubious, fly-by-night programming schools. Overarmed with high-level weapons, these roaming bands of bounty seekers hunted down and massacred the poor algorithm around the clock. The inevitable reaction occurred, but almost too late, in the form of a conservationist "Save the Algorithm" lobby, replete with badges, bumper stickers, and fund-raising algorithms. Public opinion was aroused, in particular, by a catchy campaign song:

Algorithm, algorithm, algorithm,
Who could ask for anything more?

The 1970s have brought some hope to the preservationists. Two reasonably hardy variants appear to have evolved, the *Algorithmus pascalia* and the *Algorithmus heuristicus,* which in their different ways are proving more resistant to the grosser exploitations of the unstructured. The new strains are partly the result of neo-Darwinian survival (the fitter code overcomes an antagonistic environment) and partly the outgrowth of patient, prolonged interbreeding in areas protected from bagbiters, chompers, diddlers, users, and other anathematic influences. Wirth and Knuth deserve praise in this context. The hybrid *A. seminumericalis,* for example, gently nurtured by Prof. Donald Knuth, can be spotted regularly cavorting on the sylvan campi of Stanford University, California. Its sweet, anthropomorphically cuddlesome disposition attracts weekend crowds of panda proportions. The feeding signs state quite clearly that the hybrid will not perform for peanuts; indeed, the *A. seminumericalis* needs a substantial bunch of greenery before it will embark on its dazzling repertoire of parlor tricks, delighting all age groups and both cultures. Perhaps not all, for some killjoys liken these displays of mock intelligence to the exploitation of circus animals or the chimpanzee tea party. Also, there remains the fear that, however amusing and superficially sycophantic we breed our algorithmic pets, they will prove to be feline, superior, inscrutable, and the ultimate victor.

ALLC *n.* [Association for Literary and Linguistic Computing.]   An international association founded by Prof. Roy Wisbey (King's College, London) and Mrs. Joan Smith (Regional Computing Centre, University of Manchester) to promote the use of SNOBOL.

▶Literary computing is where you can drop names as well as digits.

ALU *n.* [Arthritic Logic Unit *or* (rare) Arithmetic Logic Unit.] A random-number generator supplied as standard with all computer systems.

ancillary *adj.* [From Latin *ancilla* "maid."] *Also called* **ancilliary.** Essential.

▶As with most technical acquisitions, the primary purchase is designed to generate a growing list of essential adjuncts. Familiar domestic examples include those shown in the accompanying table.

TABLE OF ANCILLARIES

Primary purchase	Ancillaries
Movie camera	Projector, screen, splicer, splicing cement, projector stand, books of various thicknesses to adjust projector height, tolerant neighbors
Fish tank	Fish, water, heater, thermostat, thermometer(s), pebbles, pump, filter, charcoal, antichlor, replacement fish, plants, snails, lamps, more fish, fish food

The corresponding list for computers varies considerably according to type, size, and application. The environmental ancillaries are still extensive for the larger mainframes (air conditioning, false floors, standby generators, and so on), whereas the newer breeds of mini- and microsystems can be plugged in like toasters in the greasiest of kitchens. The set of ancillaries common to all DP installations contains:

A THINK SIGN

A warning sign such as the much-reproduced deterrent posted on the walls of the London University ATLAS site in the 1960s:

> ACHTUNG!!   ALLES LOOKENPEEPERS!!
>
> Das computermachine ist nicht für gefingenpoken und mittengrabben. Ist easy schnappen der springenwerk, blowenfusen und poppencorken mit spitzensparken. Ist nicht für gewerken bei das dumpkopfen. Das rubbernecken sichtseeren keepen hans in das pockets muss; relaxen und watch das blinkenlichten.

A large receptacle for discarded printouts

Several Errosol Inc.™ sprays

AND *v.trans. & adj.* **1** *v.trans.* To conjunct (several binary victims) in the boolean environment. **2** *adj.* (Of a GATE) being able to and. *Compare* NAND; NOR; OR.

ANSI *n.* [Origin: Corruption of French *ainsi* "thus" whence "ordained, obligatory." Now the presumed acronym for American National Standards Institute.] One of many national and supranational bodies devoted to establishing standards, i.e., dedicated to changing those rules which have already been universally adopted. *See also* ASCII; IBM.

aos *v.trans.* *pronounced aus* (East Coast), *ay-ahs* (West Coast)\\ [Origin: From the DEC PDP-10 increment instruction. From the JARGON FILE.] To increase the amount of something, as: "They aossed my hours but sossed my pay." *Compare* SOS.

APL *n.* [A Personal Language, A Packed Language, or (rarely) A Programming Language.] A language, devised by K. Iverson (1961), so compacted that the source code can be freely disseminated without revealing the programmer's intentions or jeopardizing proprietary rights.

♦ There are three things a man must do
Before his life is done;
Write two lines in APL,
And make the buggers run.

Apple *n.* A popular personal computer (made by Apple Computer Inc., Cupertino, California) with a refreshingly nonnumeric, non-acronymic apple-ation.

♦ I gave my love an Apple, that had no core;
I gave my love a building, that had no floor;
I wrote my love a program, that had no end;
I gave my love an upgrade, with no cryin'.

How can there be an Apple, that has no core?
How can there be a building, that has no floor?
How can there be a program, that has no end?
How can there be an upgrade, with no cryin'?

An Apple's MOS memory don't use no core!
A building that's perfect, it has no flaw!

A program with GOTOs, it has no end!
I lied about the upgrade, with no cryin'!

argument *n.* A disputatious variable constantly pouncing on innocent FUNCTIONS.

ARPA *n.* [Acronym for Advanced Research Projects Agency.] An agency of the U.S. Department of Defense established in 1968 to test its defenses against misuse and piracy in the large-scale distributed processing environment.

◗Currently, more than 200 disparate host computers at government, academic, and commercial sites are linked into the worldwide ARPA network, known as ARPANET. The results of the experiment are somewhat obscured by the fact that a few nodes slavishly observe protocol, whereas others have not yet learned how to pirate.

artificial intelligence *n. abbrev.* AI 1 The area researched by the artificial intelligentsia (attributed to Christopher Strachey (1916–1975). 2 The misguided search for a lower-unit-cost *Homo sapiens* at a time when the majority of the species remains critically underexploited [unemployed]. 3 The construction of algorithms for the blackleg assembly of wooden building-block motor cars.

ASCII *n.* [Acronym for American Standard Code for Information Interchange? Possibly from English comedian Arthur Askey.] A 7- or 8-bit code forced upon the free world by vicious anti-IBM rebels, led by the U.S. government, who held 16 card-carrying EBCDIC hostages at gunpoint in a Washington committee compound for 2 years.

◗The ASCII code, now with us like death and taxes, provides lexicographers with much-needed diversion and fun in order that "abacus," for example, can be made to precede "ZETA" in their tabulations.

ASL *n.* [American Sign Language.] A formal system of body signs for use in the nonverbal, interpersonal communications environment.

◗The DP industry offers many new employment opportunities for the disabled; indeed, computing has forced a fundamental reexamination of the traditional criteria for job discrimination on the basis of facultative impediment. Applicants with, say, chronic logismus or persistent numeriosis have always been welcomed, but we are now seeing fresh openings for those with deficiencies in the audioglottal departments. Total deafmutes, in fact, have consistently achieved top marks in the Sperry Univac

"Shut-Up-and-Listen" test. Recent ASCII extensions to ASL (see the illustration on pages 16 and 17) offer a graceful nonlinear fluency to all who are deafened by DP noise (*see* CRASH), or numbed by the semantic vacuity of a typical computer listing.

AUGRATIN *n.* [Acronym for Amalgamated Union of General Rewriters, Amenders, Tinkerers, and INterpolators.] *See* PAYROLL.

autoeroticism *n.* The computer generation of best-selling novels.

◗The Playgol package, for example, ensures the correct distribution of marketable events by line, paragraph, page, and chapter. The author simply inputs the quotas of rape, incest, bestiality, necrophilia, uralgomania, bestial rape, necrophilic incest, and so on, together with the target age group (e.g., "Under 9," "9–12 years").

The ETHELRED OS was the first to promote itself via a self-generated Robbinsesque novella called "The Ethel," of which the following extract must suffice.

Joe Spanasky stubbed out his cigarette. Another late night, he thought. Damn these Labor-saving devices. His mother had been right. He should have followed his brother Antonio into his Godfather's drug pushing syndicate in the Bronx. "Software is no kind of a job for a *man,*" Momma had cried as he boarded her private jet for London two months ago. Still, things had worked out real good, he thought. He had gained control of the British Computer Society, and his henchmen were beginning to put the screws on the members. That ballot-rigging expert from the Longshoremen's Union had done a great job . . . his next move was to quadruple the BCS dues, then the IBM UK takeover plan could move forward.

Joe lit a cigarette and glanced at the E13B numerals on his 24-carat gold Alpha wrist-watch. 23 hundred hours. The computer room downstairs would be emptying soon. All except Ethel, who would be working late. At the thought of Ethel he felt the heat surging in his loins. What a doll. A Ph.D. in statistics, and she knew all the standard deviations . . . plus a few not in the textbook. Joe stubbed out his cigarette and turned to the sleek VDU on his desk. He keyed in his secret account number and paused while the soft-green characters flashed in acknowledgement. "Tell Ethel I love her," he typed. "Sod off, don't interrupt," came the reply, almost instantaneously. Joe smiled at the low-level language and stubbed out his cigarette on the keyboard. He lit a cigarette and swivelled round to the remote air conditioning control panel. He shut down the cooling system in the computer room and gradually increased the ambient temperature rheostat. He stubbed out his cigarette and strolled to the elevator. Ignoring the signs, he lit a cigarette and stepped into the glass-walled corridors, breathing in the satisfying smoke.

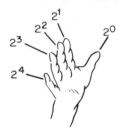

Reverse pinkie notation   Floating thumb

Unit increments in the base are indicated by clenching the fist. Touching the left ear with the right forefinger restores to binary. Tapping the Adam's apple with the left thumb signals a switch to octal. Sinistral users should add or subtract (base) ↑ 4 as the case may be, unless performing with mirrors. For IBM card messages, remember the simple rule: Nine edge leading, palms facing.

"The system has been down 10 hours."   "Overflow in register 2".

"Head crash on drum #26."

"GOTO"   "Line 1101101011."

"Logging off... see you tomorrow!"

And now, a few simple exercises:

 = ?

If  >   ELSE

Did you spot the syntax error?

autoeroticism

He stubbed out his cigarette viciously on the Tacky Mat and strode into the computer room. Ethel was leaning over the throbbing line printer. The heat was overpowering. His ploy had worked. Ethel had removed her skirt and sweater. She was straining forward on tiptoe, joggling some cards. The vibrating panels of the 401 sent cascades of ripples down her ample buttocks. Joe felt the heat surging through his loins. He took her brutally from behind, a million Think signs spinning round his head. A juicy dizziness consumed them both and a row of asterisks clattered out serially on the monitor printer. ************************************

BABOL *n.* [© Irish Business Machines.] A common language proposed to heal the endless, bloody logomachic schisms which fragment the industry. Combining the grandeur of EV-LISP and the elegance of EVQ-LISP was the primary goal.

◆BABOL may allow spurious line and statement numbers and GOTO instructions if the need to attract BASIC and FORTRAN users should arise.

backtracking *n.* The rare admission that an impasse has been reached or a deadline exceeded.

backup *n. & v. & adv.* **1** *n.* Any file, device, or person which results from backing up; the total deviance from the original is directly proportional to the number and scale of the catastrophes resulting from each copying or matching error. **2** *v.intrans.* To compound errors while merely trying to perpetuate them. **3** *v.trans.* To risk (a file, program) by attempting to copy it. **4** *v.trans.* (Of a programmer, engineer) to specify someone unacquainted with the system, job, and user. *See also* STANDBY. **5** *adv.* Annoyingly, as: "That salesman really got my backup."

ballpark *adj.* [Origin: U.S. branch of measure theory known as baseball.] **1** Deliberately underquoted, as: "The ballpark price is $25K." **2** Deliberately overquoted, as: "The printer speed varies with layout, buffer size, font repertoire, form depth, urgency, and humidity, but a ballpark figure is 500 characters per minute."

◆The basis of baseball measure theory is the analysis of input data from a series of fiscal, ballistic, gymnastic, and altercatory experiments held at ballparks each summer. The game space is divided into discrete *plays,* each of which can be reduced to about 50 numerical parameters. The definition of the measure μ on this set can be varied to produce any desired ordering of the players, teams, managers, owners, fans, and hotdog sales, e.g., player *X* has struck out more often than any other left-handed third-base Jewish Cardinal in the eighth inning of an Easter Friday road game.

base address *n.*   Low-rent accommodation of the kind frequented by operators, programmers, and other no-collar workers.

◆Even cheaper accommodation is possible—a *relative address*—if you have an aunt or an uncle living in the area.

BASIC *n.*   [Origin: *Either* acronym for Beginner's All-purpose Symbolic Instruction Code *or* Geology: *basic* "containing relatively little silica."]   Originally, a simple mid-level language used to test the student's ability to increment line numbers, but now available only in complex, extended versions. *See* EXTENDED BASIC.

◆To determine the amount of silica in your BASIC, use

INSTR(1,X$,"SILICA")

on all your strings. Scores below 5 are reassuring; scores over, say, 10 mean that you are probably using FORTRAN by mistake. Consult your supervisor at once.

Batch, Elsie   *See* DANGLING ELSE.

benchmark *v.trans.*   To subject (a system) to a series of tests in order to obtain prearranged results not available on competitive systems. *See also* MENDACITY SEQUENCE.

bends *n.pl.*   [Origin: Borrowed from sailors' slang for caisson disease.]   A painful, paralyzing, sometimes fatal dizziness caused by unseemly haste in implementing a BOTTOM-UP programming project.

besack *v.intrans.*   [Origin uncertain: possibly Russian *bez* "lacking" + ACK "a feedback signal during communications indicating acceptance."]   To engage in a prolonged monologue on diverse subjects beyond the speaker's competence and the listeners' interest. *Also called* (Brit.) **malik.**

bidirectional *adj.*   **1** (Of a printer) boustrophedonic. **2** (Of a system) being down or up. **3** (Of a consultant) able to move *toward* a prospect and *away* from a client. **4** (Of a paper- or magnetic-tape drive) able to wrench the medium from both the right- and left-hand reels.

binary *adj.*   **1** Offering little choice; maximizing the chance of error. **2** Relating to the 20th century's boring challenge to the

Babylonians. **3** Relating to a numbering system introduced to protect children from parental help during math homework assignments. **4** Reflecting the quintessential dichotomy of the universe. (*See* the table on pages 22 and 23.)

binary search *n.* A locational strategy devised by J. W. R. Dedekind (1831–1916) which worked perfectly until the advent of the file-oriented digital computer (1941–1984). The search is, in fact, misnamed since there are three possible outcomes: *not-there, wrong-find, find.* The rarity of the last explains the misnomer.

bistable *adj.* Pertaining or relating to an above-average system which is stable approximately 50 percent of the time.

bit *n. & adj.* [Origin: either Old English *bita* "something small or unimportant," or engineering *bit* "a boring tool."] **1** *n.* The quantum of misinformation. **2** *n.* One-half of the fee needed to carry out a threat, as: "For two bits I'd ram this board down your stupid throat." **3** *n.* A BINARY digit; a boringly dichotomic entity which precludes rational discussion. "Avoid situations which offer only two courses of action."—S. Murphy. **4** *adj.* (Of a programmer) inadequate; versed only in FORTRAN or RPG. **5** *adj.* (Of a map) many–1 and many–0. The 1s in a bit map indicate to the system those sectors of mass memory which are immune from further corruption.

bit bucket *n.* [Origin: possibly (vulg.) Cockney rhyming slang.] **1** A binary spittoon. **2** A digital cuspidor.

◗Bit buckets are analogous to the receptacles fitted in the back of high-priced television sets to catch the corpses of cowboys and indians. Without a well-placed bit bucket to collect overflow characters as they are coughed up from stretched stacks and raucous registers, an offensive GRUNGE accumulates beneath the computer cabinets. This binary detritus, if left to fester, can be a hazard to operational health and efficiency.

blank card *n. Also called* **spacer card.** An unpunched card placed in an input deck at 10,000-card intervals. Since electromechanical devices enjoy a consistent 1-10^4 error rate, the blank-card trick minimizes the impact of card-reader malfunctions.

◗The Zen representative at the ISO (International Standards Organization) has proposed that certain card-punching conventions be observed to avoid the present confusion between space, blank, null, and "not there." It does seem helpful to have a positive "not there" column code so that *missing* columns and cards—the erstwhile bane of unit recorders

BINARY TABLE

Element 0	Element 1
True	False
IBM	The seven dwarfs
Good	Cheap
Black	White
Pro	Con
Even	Odd
Flop	Flip
+	−
Female	Piggish
Batch	Waiting
Finite	Interesting
Order	Cancellation
Up	Crashed
"X"	But, having said "X," . . .
Me	You
West	North, south, and east
Here and there	Neither here nor there
Local	Informed
Error	Undetected error
FORTRAN	Elegance
Structured	Wrong
Working	Promised
Published	Rejected
Loved	Dead
Prime	Old
Prime	Factorable
Payable	Disputed
Disputed	Receivable
Filed	Safe
Recidivism	Monocidivism
Civilization	Los Angeles
Floppy disk	Storage

Element 0	Element 1
Dodger	Giant
Big bang	Steady squib
One-liner	Shaggy-dog
Redbrick	Cambridge
Snow culture 1	Snow culture 2
Minmax	Maxmin
You name it	Null
The principle of duality	The principle of duality
Other things being equal	Nevertheless
This	That
This'n'that	Other
Headword	Undefinable
Wagnerian	Philistine
High-level	FORTRAN
FORTRAN	Nontransportable
Science	Computer science
The set of all sets which are not members of themselves	$\sim(x:\forall x.x \notin x)$
Unwanted	Paged
On sale	Marked down
Basic	Extended
Economical	Achievable
1	0

—can be punched and verified before input. Perforatricial productivity payment schemes, which traditionally penalize columnar oversights, would reward sins of omission and commission with equal severity. The Zen convention demands that each blank card be punched and verified (a total of 160 keystrokes), but whether a missing blank card requires this effort or not is still subject to intense mootation.

block *n. & v.trans.* **1** *n.* The place of execution. **2** *v.trans.* To hinder (a user, job, program) by changing the password or improving the operating system. **3** *v.trans.* To interject control characters at arbitrary points (in a message) prior to transmission.

blockhead *n.* The first character foolish enough to venture into a VTAM applications program.

bonus *n. Also called* **added bonus.** [Latin *bonus* "good."] **1** *n. Payroll* A random amount added to the net pay to compensate for random withholding errors. **2** Any unexpected, additional benefit encountered or offered when all seems to be going well.

◗The superstitious, i.e., experienced, DP person dreads and shuns all added bonuses. They are known as portents of 12th-hour revenge and disaster in nonadjacent modules. Thus:

> "Finishing the stock update by 3:00 P.M. provides the *added bonus* of two extra hours on the Fixed Asset Depreciation Schedule."

> "If you order the additional 16K RAM, you get the *added bonus* of three days free tuition in BASIC from one of our extended counselors."

> "Our book club will save you up to 40 percent off normal retail price, and as a *bonus,* your name will be passed to 98 carefully selected mailing lists."

bootstrap *n. & v.trans* [Origin: from the fictional attempts by Baron Münchhausen (described by Rudolf Raspe, 1785) to refute Newton's third law. Subsequent real bids at self-levitation led to the disappearence of straps from the footwear environment.] **1** *n.* The first straw that breaks the system's back. **2** *v.trans. Also called* **boot** To ensnare (an operating system or program) in a sneaky, cumulative manner.

◗The thought that a cold system needs to read in the read-in subroutine before it can read in anything has kept countless amateur ontogenists and etiologists from the arms of Morpheus since the dawn of cybernetic consciousness. The practical DP pioneers chickened out of this infinite regress by laying a golden egg, to wit, a bootstrap.

bottom-down *adj.* [© Irish Business Machines.] Relating to a pessimistic and discredited programming methodology.

◗Bottom-down projects are characterized by deep-rooted doubts as to where to start, and by a signal lack of progress once started. *Compare* BOTTOM-UP; MIDDLE-OUT; TOP-DOWN.

bottom line *n.* The 24th line on a typical VDU, reserved for error messages. This convention is also used on balance sheets and other financial reports.

bottom-up *adj.* Relating to a programming methodology in which the finer details are coded before any study of the overall needs of the system has been made.

♦Historically, the bottom-up approach replaced the less optimistic BOTTOM-DOWN strategy, only to be challenged by the TOP-DOWN philosophy. A recent Taoist revolution bids fair to replace all three with the MIDDLE-OUT credo. Project coordinators still working in the bottom-up environment face the happy task of blending a cornucopia of well-written but mutually contradictory submodules. The ideal bottom-up coordinator should be a top-downer at heart, able to dive in before any of the team have surfaced, meet them at three fathoms or less, and gain control of their oxygen control valves. *See also* BENDS.

breakpoint *n.* 1 A situation in which the system and the programmer are tied after a certain number of runs and the winner is decided by a sudden-death series of DUMPS. 2 The delightful but self-defeating moment when the DPM dismisses the entire systems/programming team, the user rejects the supplier, and four overextended legal partnerships meet to berate the litigious fervor of their respective clients. 3 A line in a program highlighted by the clairvoyant and dubious.

broket *n.* [Origin: by analogy with "bracket," a broken bracket. From JARGON FILE.] *Also called* **angle bracket.** Either of the characters " < " and " > ."

bubble memory *n.* A storage device developed by South Sea Memory Products Inc.

♦The chief advantage of bubbles over floppies is that they cannot be folded by the mailman. Whether bubbles will ever replace the hard disk (which is also beyond the bending power of most postal workers) depends on the relative strength of the semiconductor and metallurgical lobbies.

bubble sort *n.* A program for arranging memory bubbles in any desired sequence (by diameter, mass, viscosity, manufacturer, cost, etc.).

buffer *n.* [Origin obscure: possibly Italian *buffo* "farcical, comic" or Latin *bufo* "a toad."] 1 A region between two devices designed to distort or, if possible, prevent the flow of data in either direction. 2 An old, greasy, and abrasive rag used to clean tape heads.

bug *n.* [Entomology obscure.] 1 An undocumented feature. 2 A mythical scapegoat invoked by all sections of the DP industry: "A pox on the bug and a bug on the pox, for one or t'other plagues my TOS."—Sir John Thumpstaff.

◖The word implies that "things go wrong" because of some infection from outside. The *gremlin* which caused all malfunctions during World War II was an openly fictitious imp, blamed in jest; the DP bug, however, has assumed the unfunny proportions of an infestation. Putting things right, or debugging, therefore, requires the equivalent of fumigation, chlorination, swabbing, or, to use the proper chemotherapeutic terminology, "nailing the little bastards." That the epidemic persists would indicate that there are terminal diseases beyond the remedial arts of computer science. The ailing user is often advised to "keep taking the tablets and see how you feel in the morning." The patient must accept the palliative KLUDGE or the placebo of a MAJOR NEW-LEVEL RELEASE. Since, in truth, most DP errors arise from sins of omission, rather than commission, the appropriate medical analogy to the DP bug is not infection but metabolic disorder or vitamin deficiency.

bundled *adj.* [From the verb *bundle* "to throw together in haphazard fashion."] Of or relating to an arbitrary collection of software items offered as seen, without charge or warranty, to certain prospects in a competitive environment.

◖Of interest to sociolinguists is the fact that the DP usage of *bundled* was triggered by the prior introduction of the antonym *unbundled* by IBM the previous day. *See* UNBUNDLING.

bus *n.* A ponderous vehicle for transporting people or data at irregular intervals.

◖Note, however, that "missing the bus" has opposite connotations in the people and data environments: a failure for folk, but a blessing for bits. Of the contending mini- and microbus formats, the ruthless, teutonic SS-100 standard is certain to dominate. As the name suggests, a task force of highly motivated "standards specialists" regularly descends upon nonconforming stockists, outside of normal trading hours, and throws some rather exegetical pitches. Few can resist the board-crunching logic of these visits.

CAD *n.* [Acronym for Computer-Aided Delay or, *archaic,* Computer-Aided Design.] The automation of the traditionally *manual* delays between the various stages of product development: research and development, drawing office, prototyping, testing, preproduction planning, etc. The improved delays invariably lead to better products.

CAI *n.* [Computer-Aided Instruction.] The misguided attempt to replace each teacher in the Bronx with 60 on-line terminals. *Compare* CAL.

CAL *n.* [Acronym for CALifornia or, *archaic,* Computer-Aided Learning.] A superior West Coast (U.S.A.) version of CAI in which each teacher is replaced by 25 on-line terminals.

call *n.* [Origin: theater, as in traditional request "Five minutes, darling!"] A polite but unheeded plea for help from one piece of troubled coding to another. Subsequent, less polite, calls are known as *screams. See also* GOSUB.

campus *n.* [Latin *campus* "field (of battle)."] An area of scholastic and riotous endeavor offering students their first real opportunity to freak a large timesharing system. *See also* RESPONSE TIME.

card *n. Also called* **punch card, punched card, tab card, Hollerith card.** [Origin: from earlier, more predictable games of chance and necromantic divination.] A 7⅜-inch × 3¼-inch looseleaf scratchpad system designed to fit normal shirt pockets (other sizes are available for the abnormal), but sometimes underused as an 80 × 12 analog-digital matrix. "If T. J. Watson, Sr., had played his cards right, he could have made his name in computing."—M. Thumps.

◆The optimum size of the 80-column card is a strange accident arising from the parsimony of Dr. Herman Hollerith, who wanted a cheap filing system for his card-based census of 1890. He therefore designed his card to fit the filing trays available, which were based on the dimensions of the 1890 dollar bill. The latter, naturally, had been created with standard wallet and shirt-pocket sizes in mind. Despite the ravages of inflation, Herman's card survives. Rival formats come and go, but nothing can budge the diehard chemisier.

card, blank *n.* *See* BLANK CARD.

catastrophe *n.* *See* SEVEN CATASTROPHES OF COMPUTING, THE.

CEU *n.* [Continuing Education Unit]   One of a sequence of random integers issued in a version of keno known as *adult education.*

◆Players achieving certain preordained totals are required to yell "Ex-tra curr-i-cu-la!" before claiming their diplomas in such diverse fields as brain surgery, intermediate mollusk sexing, and hierarchical data structures for the small business user.

Participating readers who have successfully reached this page are entitled to deduct two CEUs from their accumulated tally.

chad *n.* (plural **chadim**)   A piece of confetto produced by a tape or card punch.

chadless tape *n.*   Paper tape prepared on a punch with blunt pins. *See also* CHAD.

Chain *or* **Cha'n, Daisy.** *See* DAISY CHAIN.

Chinese remainder theorem *n.*   More strictly, a *conjecture* that there exists an $N \geq 3$ such that after World War N the set of surviving Chinese will be nonempty. A corollary asserts that for $N + 1$ the set will be less nonempty. If the set is exhausted after M trials, we define World War M as the War to end all conjectures.

◆United States and Soviet nuclear strategy is so heavily based on this conjecture that many computer simulations to test its validity have been attempted. These models have, so far, proved to be inconclusive and expensive, and there is mounting pressure to divert the Pentagonal OR budget into more reliable, practical experiments.

Chinese total *n.*   **1** Almost a billion. **2** A checksum methodology originally devised for YODALS (Yangtse Opium Den Accounts Leceivable System), whence often referred to as a *hash total.* *Also called* (mainly in China) a Russian or Czech total.

Chinese VMOS *n.* For full details, please consult the Yellow Pages. *See* NETWOK; VMOS.

close *adj. & v.* **1** *adj.* Relating to the nearest possible approach to project completion. *See* HARTREE CONSTANT. **2** *v.trans.* To protect (a file) until the next OPEN statement. **3** *v.intrans.* To invoke the "File not open" diagnostic.

closed *adj.* **1** (Of a fist) showing a complete lack of budgetary imagination, but prepared to counter accusations of parsimony with pugilistic rebuttal. **2** (Of a topological set) lacking candor. **3** (Of a shop) Brit.: requiring job-unrelated qualifications. **4** (Of a file) safe. **5** (Of a loop) narcissistic; obsessed with its own parameters. *Compare* OPEN.

COBOL *n.* [Origin obscure: possibly from *cobble* "to botch" or *cobbing* "a way to punish sailors." Now assumed acronym for **CO**mmon **B**usiness **O**riented **L**anguage.] A procedurally disoriented language pioneered by Commander Grace Murray Hopper of the U.S. Navy. In keeping with naval tradition, a tot of rum is still forced down the throats of reluctant middy COBOL programmers before they swab their daily deck of cards.

code *v.intrans.* To resort, reluctantly, to the CODING phase of the programming cycle. *See* MURPHY'S LAW OF PROGRAMMING.

coding *n.* The setting up of a 1-1 relationship between ENDLESS LOOPS on a FLOWCHART and endless loops in a PROGRAM.

collective noun *n.* "A singularly euphonious appellation."—W. C. Fields. A revealing name applied to a class or aggregate, as: "a pride of lexicographers," "a doze of profredders." *See* the table on page 30.

combinatorial explosion *n.* [Origin: *combination* "nethergarment" + *explosion.*] **1** The limit, as $N \to \infty$, of

$$C = N!/(N - [e^i])!$$

where N is the number of fresh underwear items available each day, i is the factor of incontinency, and C is the number of unmentionable possibilities. **2** The inescapable fate of all nontrivial computer systems. The neo-Luddites may get them first.

come from *n.* An instruction proposed by R. Lawrence Clark (1973) to resolve the GOTO controversy. The industry is still (1981) bristling with acute disbelief.

TABLE OF COLLECTIVE NOUNS

Unit member	Collective noun(s)
Field engineer	An *absence* of field engineers
User	A *bleat* of users
	or A *jury* of users
Manufacturer	A *dock* of manufacturers
DPM	A *panic* of DPMs
Systems analyst	An *expectation* of systems analysts
Programmer	A *detail* of programmers
Operator	An *indifference* of operators
Salesperson	A *trough* of salespersons
Consultant	A *retreat* of consultants
Deadline	A *sequence* of deadlines
Connector	A *conspiracy* of connectors
Dump	A *gloom* of dumps
String	A *vest* of strings
Crash	A *jangle* of crashes
Datum	A *loss* of data
High-level language	A *logomachy* of high-level languages
	or A *babol* of high-level languages
Competitor	A *rafter* of competitors
Senior COBOL programmer	A *load* of old Cobollers

common language *n.*   1 A language used only by the originator and his/her closest friends. 2 A grandiose scheme launched by Friden Inc. in the late 1950s to provide a paper-tape Esperanto linking all known data preparation and processing devices.

▶In spite of some initial success, the users' intense desire to be different led to a plethora of incompatible dialects, and the experiment foundered between the Scylla of three tape widths, two chadic states, five opaquacities, and a whole ferranti of coding variations, and the Charybdis of IBM's selfish allegiance to the CARD. *See also* BABOL.

compatable *adj.* *Also* (in *archaic* systems literature) **compatible.** Pertaining to a supposed relationship between a given set of existing characteristics (known as the "installed set") and a mooted, nonexisting set (known as the "proposed set").

◆Current DP usage allows a variety of colorful qualifications to the basic concept of compatability, including many adverbs of motion, e.g., upward, downward, sideways, recessively. Degrees of compatability are rated 1 to 10 on the Richter scale, but the measurement, so far, lacks solid scientific objectivity. For example, when the supplier of the proposed set is a competitor of the supplier of the installed set, the two suppliers' assessments have been known to differ by as much as nine Richter points. Many experienced upgraders, in fact, are opposed to *any* partial qualifications of the predicate, such as "almost compatable," "as good as compatable," "compatable except on a set of measure zero," and so on. The side effects of near "compatability," they claim, are infinitely more horrendous than those of total inconsistency.

compatible *adj.*   Chiefly *archaic* spelling of **compatable.**

◆Beware of the **compatible** variant, which indicates that the proposal was written by non-DP staff.

complex *n. & adj.*   **1** *n.* Any system, subsystem, sub-subsystem, etc., which is priced as a separate item in a proposal, as: "The head office 6×4-1100 will be in a real-time on-line situation with each branch. The branch-office *complex* comprises 1 (one) teleprinter and modem." **2** *adj.* (Of a DP problem) resolvable into two parts: a real part which can be solved or shelved, and an imaginary part which requires a complete and immediate restructuring of the DP department.

comprise *v.trans.(?) and/or intrans.(?)* (Mandatory DP usage) to consist: "The system comprises of the following items"; "the system is comprised with the following items."

◆Beware of proposals using the archaic phrasal verb *consist of.* Compare COMPATIBLE.

computable *adj.*   Chiefly *archaic* spelling of **computible.** *Compare* COMPATABLE.

◆The theoretical foundations of "computability" were exhausted by Turing and others in the mid/late 1930s and might have remained as a branch of pure mathematics had not Hitler challenged the military strength of Oxford, Cambridge, Harvard, and Princeton. From 1938 to 1946, the μ-recursive function was armed with sticky relays, glowing tubes, dry joints, and mercurious delay lines to implement the still undersung *Win World War II* package. Fascism, having alienated the best programmers, could not match the Allied ballistic, nuclear, logistic, and, perhaps of most value, cryptanalytic computational resources. (Ronald Lewin, *Ultra Goes to*

War, McGraw-Hill, New York, 1978.) Lest we forget . . . when you next run StarTrader, Hammurabi, or Battleships on your playful inhouse system, spare a thought for those who computed a real war, and won: Atanasoff, Bigelow, Churchhouse, J. P. Eckert, W. J. Eckert, Einstein, Fermi, Goldstine, Mauchly, Newman, Oppenheimer, Telford, Turing, Ulam, von Neumann, Welchman, . . .

computer journalist *n.* A programmer or systems analyst lured into the tabloid cesspool with false promises of shorter hours, better pay, and less attention to detail. The unsatisfied craving for an audience often leads to an early return to the former honest labors.

computer music *n.* 1 The sudden burst of silence when you switch off. 2 Any polyhedral, noncelestial approximation to spherical harmonics. *See also* SAWTEETH.

computer science *n.* [Origin: possibly Prof. P. B. Fellgett's rhetorical question, "Is computer science?"] 1 A study akin to numerology and astrology, but lacking the precision of the former and the success of the latter. 2 The protracted value analysis of algorithms. 3 The costly enumeration of the obvious. 4 The boring art of coping with a large number of trivialities. 5 Tautology harnessed in the service of Man at the speed of light. 6 The Post-Turing decline in formal systems theory. "Science is to computer science as hydrodynamics is to plumbing."—Prof. M. Thümp.

♦The only universally accepted computer scientific theorem to emerge, so far, is my own rather depressing:

Theorem: *All programs are dull.*

Proof: Assume the contrary; i.e., the set of interesting programs is nonempty. Arrange them (or it) in order of interest (note that all sets can be well ordered, so do it properly). The minimal element is the *least interesting program,* the obvious dullness of which provides the contradictory denouement we so devoutly seek.

Some plagiarists have tried to reverse this argument to show that all programs are interesting, but all they actually prove is that there exists a *least dull program.* This I am willing to accept, since I wrote it in 1954 —and I can assure you that it is no longer of any interest to me or anyone.

computible *adj. Also* (in *archaic* systems literature) **computable.** (Of a function) listed, or claimed to be listed, in any extant manufacturer's catalog of available software.

congress *n.* [From Latin *com* "together" + *grădătĭo* "climax" *or* Sanskrit *(Kama Sutra)* "intercourse between Indians of disparate endowments."]   A wild CONVENTION.

conjecture *n.*   1 *Mathematics* A hypothesis in search of a counterexample. Once united, they marry, move to the suburbs, raise a few boring lemmata, and are never heard of again.

▶Some conjectures, alas, seem doomed to sail forever seeking conjugal resolution, allowed to come ashore but once a year. They anchor briefly near the Martin Gardner strands until the smooth rabble drives them out to sea.

2 *Data processing* The firm, irrevocable, notarized pledge, sworn on the grave of one or both of the programmer's putative parents, that the job will run on time (excluding any delays caused or enhanced by war, civil commotion, or rioting, whether declared, spontaneous, reprehensible, or justified; undue pressure to perform, from whatsoever source; mal de mer, mal de pays, mal de siècle, mal de code, mal de machine, or any force majeure not pretofore invoked).

▶Embarrassed with a daily richness of firm conjectures, the DPM is left with a pleasantly selective task known as scheduling.

console *n.* [From Latin *consolatio(n)* "comfort, spiritual solace."]   A device for displaying or printing condolences and obituaries for the OPERATOR.

▶   Randomly accessed my girl is delirious;
I even consoled her one night on the Sirius;
The monitor printer did then overswing;
It took away one of my favorite things!

consultant *n.* [From *con* "to defraud, dupe, swindle," or, possibly, French *con* (vulgar) "a person of little merit" + *sult* elliptical form of "insult."]   A tipster disguised as an oracle, *especially* one who has learned to decamp at high speed in spite of the large briefcase and heavy wallet.

▶The earliest literary reference appears to be the ninth-century Arabic tale *Ali Baba and the Forty Consultants*.

convention *n.* [From Latin *convĕnire* "to come together."]   An alibi; saturnalia; a gathering held at a safe distance from one's family; a place where normal behavioral conventions are suspended. *See also* CONGRESS; SYMPOSIUM.

33

conversion *n.* [Latin *conversare* "to turn around frequently."] The regular, major recasting of one's software and databases to avoid the stigma of OBSOLESCENCE. *See also* UPGRADE.

correctrice *n.* [Feminine form of French *correcteur* "profredder."] A French preuf reeader with MIDDLEWARE and dyslexia.

cpm *n.* [Charlatans Per Minute.] *Queuing theory* The arrival rate of salespersons, indicating the number of mailing lists to which the visitee has been exposed.

CPU *n.* [*Chiefly archaic* abbreviation for Central Processing Unit.] The calculating mill that Babbage dreamed on.

◆The dream was eventually realized in the 1950s, but is now being replaced by a diffused continuum of minute noncomputing elements known as MICROPROCESSORS.

crash *n. & v.* **1** *n.* *Software* An audible warning that it's DOWNTIME time again.

◆In excessively unstable environments the warnings combine to give the illusion of a continuous tone, e.g., middle C for Exec 8, A♭ above middle C for OS/360, and so on, but cases have been reported in which the human audio range has been exceeded. Some Chronos II sites have specially trained watchdogs to alert the operator. The legendary St. Paul Breakpointer, it is claimed, not only whines suggestively *before* the system dies, but also points at the offending line of code.

2 *n.* *Hardware* The distinctive sound made by drums and disks when heads drop.

◆Head crashes serve to resolve fundamental problems in maintaining dynamic equilibrium while the head is aquaplaning over the ill-defined magnetic oxide impurities which sometimes accumulate on the drum or disk surface. These rustlike layers are not intrinsically harmful—indeed, some claim that they actually protect the costly metal below—but they can acquire spurious, palimpsestuous images, known variously as tracks, sectors, or records. If the normal head burnishing action fails to correct these aberrations, a head crash is initiated, signaled by a triumphant rasp (the French call it "un pet de soulagement"). Well-designed drum/disk subsystems will demagnetize the surface before removing the fetid strata. Many variants are available: read after crash, crash before write, crash after crash, etc.

3 *v.trans.* To put down (a system or device). **4** *v.intrans.* (Of people) to lapse suddenly into a state of intense abulia, *especially* at vital moments during a highly structured walk-through.

▶Typical crash triggers are voices (including your own) announcing that (1) "We now need to look at the **DMS** sub-sub-subschema definitions"; (2) "When I took over the payroll package maintenance responsibility 12 years ago. . . ."

Creed *n.* A very early, dogmatic teleprinter.

▶ When they put the Apostles' Creed in,
It was soon replaced by Friden;
St. Peter has the system well in hand;
There's a name tape sent from Hell
In the ATR as well,
Typing letters of condolence to the Damned.

CRT *n.* [Cathode Ray Tube.] Originally an important storage device, developed by Prof. F. C. Williams, Manchester University, in 1947, but now relegated to trivial applications in the timesharing and entertainment environments. *See also* GLASS TTY.

cursor *n.* [Possibly Old Irish *cursagim* "to blame" or English *cursory* "rapid, superficial."] A faintly flickering symbol on a CRT screen, used to test the eyesight and reflexes of the operator, and indicating where the next keyed character will be rejected.

▶In parts of England frustrated terminal minders often refer to the *blinking* cursor. A cursor in the top left-hand position of an otherwise blank screen serves to indicate that the system (with the exception of the cursor-generation module) is inoperative. In well-designed systems the cursor flicker rate is set to match the operator's alpha brain rhythm to provide an inescapably hypnotic point of interest until normal service is resumed.

The record for loyal patience belongs to the late M. Thumps, whose atrophied corpse was discovered slumped over a remote terminal of the British Rail TRAIN (Train Recovery And Identification Network)* complex 2 years after his particular line had been closed. The postmortem, performed by Terminal Diseases Inc., proudly revealed that the cursor was still flashing, a fact subsequently exploited in the manufacturer's gruesomely effective advertising campaign. Who will want to forget the full-page picture of the remains of Mr. Thump's index finger, pitifully poised above the GO key? TOPE (the Terminal OPerators' Executive) has converted Signal Box 327, Camden Town, London, into a permanent museum-shrine in honor of Micky Thumps. A blue plaque outside bears the epitaph:

---

*Initiated following the Great Train Robbery of 1895 but not fully operational until after the Great Train Robbery of 1963.

Young Mick stood by the empty screen
Whence all but he had fled;
In vain he waited for response,
Now, like the line, he's dead.

Inside, a tastefully cobwebbed replica of Thump's putrefied cadaver, erected by public subscription, can be seen seated at the silent, inexorable CRT, symbolizing the stubborn, pigheaded pride of the timesharer whom time has passed by. Inserting a coin of modest denomination into an adjacent slot, the pilgrim is rewarded with a macabre reenactment of Thumps's final attempts to logon. Bony fingertips scratch the keytops, the cursor blinks but does not move, and a crescendo of bleeps drowns poor Thumps's last modest screams of despair.

cursor address *n.*   "Hello, cursor!"

curtation *n.*   The enforced compression of a string in the fixed-length field environment.

▶The problem of fitting extremely variable-length strings such as names, addresses, and item descriptions into fixed-length records is no trivial matter. Neglect of the subtle art of curtation has probably alienated more people than any other aspect of data processing. You order Mozart's *Don Giovanni* from your record club, and they invoice you $24.95 for MOZ DONG. The witless mapping of the sublime onto the ridiculous! Equally puzzling is the curtation that produces the same eight characters: THE BEST, whether you order *The Best of Wagner, The Best of Schubert,* or *The Best of the Turds.* Similarly, wine lovers buying from computerized wineries twirl their glasses, check their delivery notes, and inform their friends, "A rather innocent, possibly overtruncated CAB SAUV 69 TAL." The squeezing of fruit into 10 columns has yielded such memorable obscenities as COX OR PIP.

The examples cited are real, and the curtational methodology which produced them is still with us. *Compare* TRUNCATE.

Daisy Chain *or* **Cha'n** (1831–1895). Legendary Bangkok prostitute-inventor who developed and gave her name to several anachronistic communications and printing devices.

◖She left for the United States in 1879 ("breaking all my Thais," as she put it) and became Herman Hollerith's mistress-assistant at the Census Office. She died there in 1895 during an all-night card-joggling session. Her son, Markov, took his mother's surname, but did not inherit her practical, electromechanical skills. However, Markov soon showed signs of genius as a pure mathematician, and his pioneering work in the theory of stochastic processes probably helped Dr. Hollerith more than any of his mother's futuristic peripherals. Mystery surrounds the fate of Markov Chain. His evening walks became more and more erratic, and one night he simply failed to come home.

Dr. Hollerith tried, unsuccessfully, to incorporate Daisy's ideas into his hardware. Her line printer called for a horizontally rotating band on which were set, at regular intervals, 80 small windmill-like devices, free to spin in a vertical plane, each carrying 96 printing elements, one at each tip of the windmill's vanes. Hollerith spent 5 years digesting the previous sentence, and a further 5 on the inertial and timing problems of his prototype. Although he never broke the 1 line per minute barrier, he accidentally—some 20 years before Sikorsky—built a 2-ton monster that could hover 6 inches above floor level. Dr. Hollerith's dying words, in 1929, were: "On mein Herz you vill find ze werd, *Gänseblümchenketterdrucker.*"

Dangling Else [Posthumous hypocorism for **Elsie Batch** (1940–1974).]

◖A pioneer Pascal blaise-trailer who committed suicide after a particularly frustrating session with her primitive compiler. Her ghost is reputed to lurk yet around the computer room at North Staffs Polytechnic (Staffordshire, England), where her vengeful spirit is blamed for any otherwise

unaccountable system crash. Her tombstone in the Shrewesbury Bone
Orchard bears the following salutary epitaph:

"Poor Dangling Else!," her fellow users cried;
To cut her down and vet her source they tried.
"**IF** only she had double-checked," they whooped,
"Her neck would not be unconditionally looped!
"Her once soft eyes would not be swollen
"**ELSE** had she spied the missing semicolon!
"Her timeshared lips would still be smiling;
"Alas, she now lies decompiling!"

Dear Pascal users who pass by,
O **PAUSE** a **WHILE**, and heed my cry.
No **ARGUMENT** can bring me back
And without **Wirth,** true **Worth** I lack!
My tragic **CASE** should make **AMEND;**
BEGIN a-**NEW,** avoid my **END!**

FOR careless coding in the young
Can leave a program, and a body, **HUNG!**

data *n.* [Latin *dăre* "to offer or give," whence *dătum* "that which is
offered or given."] The singular collective noun for a set of
datums.

◗Mandatory DP usage has *data* in the singular, without exception: "The
data is punched and verified." The singularity of *data* is powerful enough
to override preceding pluralities, as: "Ten thousand cards of data is
punched and verified." Proposals or documents with such flashy affecta-
tions as, "Having been punched, the data are verified," are invariably
dismissed as the work of pettifogging technical writers who wouldn't
know a data if they tripped over it. Similar pitfalls exist in the spoken
environment, although the rules are more flexible. The choice between
darter, dayter, and *datter* (rarely, *darrer*) will depend, in a most subtle manner,
on the longitude of the speaker and the latitude of the audience. The
received classical phonetic canon indicates the shortest vowel, but there
are many gaps in our knowledge of Roman computing practice. When in
doubt, a safe alternative pronunciation is *in-form-ay-shun,* provided that
you are not addressing a convention of full-time semanticists. The latter
incline to the view that *information* is that which is left *after* data has been
processed, but the practical computerperson cannot afford to be so pessimistic.
   A more fundamental attack on the validity of *data,* as used by the DP
industry, has come recently from the eminent Scandinavian etymologist,

Prof. M. Thumpersen. Thumpersen argues that computer science, being new, undisciplined, and lacking any widely accepted central authority in charge of nomenclature, has borrowed naïvely from other, more precise taxonomies. He claims, in particular, that the key word *data* is a grotesque misnomer, since computer data is never "given" and seldom "offered." Thumpersen urges a move to the more appropriate (cãpio, capĕre, cēpi, captum) roots, i.e., a switch from the "giving" implied by *data* to the "taking" suggested by *capta.* To encourage the adoption of such phrases as *capta entry, capta processing, captabase,* and *Capta General Inc.,* he is prepared to accept that *capta* is treated as a singular noun. "It would be unrealistic," Thumpersen explained, "to expect too dramatic a change in CP usage."

data bank *n.* A place where DATA can be deposited with the traditional security associated with financial institutions, such as Equity Funding Corporation of America, IOS, and Franklyn National, to name but three.

◗Data bank interest can vary, but usually peaks at the moment of retrieval. As with coitus interruptus, there are substantial penalties for late withdrawal.

Database Management System *n. Also* DBMS. [Origin: DATA + Latin *basus* "low, mean, vile, menial, degrading, counterfeit."] 1 *Marketing* Any filing system. 2 *Software* A complex set of interrelational data structures, allowing data to be lost in many convenient sequences while retaining a complete record of the logical relations between the missing items.

DBMS *n.* DATABASE MANAGEMENT SYSTEM.

deadline *n.* 1 *Communications* A NACKered line that rejects all handshakes, however friendly. 2 *Scheduling* One of a sequence of vague prophecies; a given date before which assignments must not be completed. *See also* HARTREE CONSTANT.

debugger *n.* (Anglo-Irish) The person responsible for errors in a program; the person who sold us our system.

debugging *n.* Removing a BUG, either by tinkering with the program or by amending the program specification so that the side effect of the bug is published as a desirable feature. *See also* KLUDGE; ONE-LINE PATCH; STEPWISE REFINEMENT.

◗Fixing one's own errors is such a hazardous and humiliating process that programmers are well advised to observe the Kelly-Bootle Rule: "Avoid debugging! Get it right the first time!" Correcting the work of others, though, has its lighter moments, for it is difficult to suppress the occasional wry chuckle (pronounced *Yahooo!*) as your colleague's blatant howlers are methodically exposed and neatly patched. *See* YOUR PROGRAM.

decade counter *n.* A slow real-time clock used in automated news media offices. Every 10 years a signal is generated to initiate a spate of retrospection and prediction.

▶The best-known example, perhaps, is JANUS (JANuary Updating Service), which provides an annual subpulse. This trigger creates a hierarchical database of the previous year's nonevents and a selection of the more idle speculations on the year to come. The 10-year (or *decadent*) clock pulse invokes a complex collation of the previous files from which the presses and TV cameras can roll out the spiritual distillation of the ($n \times 10$)'s.

decision table *n.* **1** A choice between the noise of the cabaret and the smell of the kitchen. **2** A noncomputable variant of tic-tac-toe.

decompiler *n.* **1** (Brooklyn English) the compiler. **2** The software needed to undo the wrongs of compilation, i.e., to repack object worms in a can of source.

decompiling, James Joyce's law of "What's source for the goose is object for the gander."

default *n.* [Possibly from Black English "De fault wid dis system is you, man."] **1** The vain attempt to avoid errors by inactivity. "Nothing will come of nothing: speak again."—*King Lear*. **2 default option.** A soft option.

▶The default option is always worth a try when in doubt. The system tries to guess what you really want, and, even if it guesses wrong, at least the whole transaction is legal syntactically. Furthermore, you have a credible scapegoat, which, nowadays, is sure hard to find.

degrade *v.trans.* **1** To add a terminal to (a timesharing system). **2** To promote (a programmer) to systems analyst.

delay *n.* **1** The elapsed time between successive deadlines. **2** A period of frustrating inactivity so fatal in all its consequences that no member of the DP community can relax until every single manifestation has been tracked down, identified, and stored in the pending file.

▶*Compare* PAUSE.

denier *n.* [Origin: possibly French *dénier* "to refuse to recognize."] A proposed unit of string coarseness which has yet to gain ISO/ASCII approval.

‣The measure assigns *zero* to the NULL string, *one* to benign strings (such as "God bless you," "Sláinte," etc.), and *infinity* to any string containing "*****"

depilation *n.* [Latin *de* "away" + *pilus* "hair."] The painful process whereby programs are made less HAIRY.

‣A DP trickopathist writes: "One of life's most enduring and remunerative paradoxes is that, for every patient I have complaining of a superfluity in the trichoid environment, I can cite and bill another with the contrary affliction. Hair, or the lack of it, it seems, always looks greener on the other side. Some programmers worry unduly when their programs become *more* hairy in spite of long sessions aimed at simplification. We in the trade call this "the third-shift shadow" problem. I advise such patients, regardless of sex, to relax, step aside from the job, retire to bed with a cheap novel, and sip my guaranteed medication. There are some horripilations, of course, beyond the grasp of trichopathy, and for those in a seriously deep trichoma we can do little more than find a scapegoat and a change of scenery.

"Hair deficiency, on the other hand or chest, can always be remedied, either by natural methods (usually by a fresh, more realistic assessment of the problem to be programmed) or by artificial complexifications. The latter techniques range from the grafting of hair to hide any thin patches of triviality, to the fitting of a global program toupee able to give to the most mundane package unimpeachable profundity and daunting opaqueness. A full refund is made if anyone spots the join!"

dismal *adj.* [Origin: malapropistic transformation of *decimal* "pertaining to or founded on the number 10."] **1** *Currency* Boring; lacking the traditional, sterling, and natural basal variety of a mixed duodecimal and vicenary monetary system. **2** *Adders* Not quite reliable: "In fact, we dubbed it the 'dismal' adder because of its proximity to the edge of workability."—Herman Lukoff, *From Dits to Bits*, Robotics Press, 1979.

documentation *n.* [Latin *documentum* "warning."] **1** The promised literature that fails to arrive with the supporting hardware. **2** A single, illegible, photocopied page of proprietary caveats and suggested infractions. **3** The detailed, unindexed description of a superseded package.

dope *n.* The Philosopher's Stone of electronic alchemy.

♦Cynics have noted the cussedness of 20th-century alchemy, in which a deliberate impurity (or fix) transmutes pure silicon into base transistors.

double-sided drum *n.* [ⓒ Irish Business Machines.] A discontinued device aimed at storing data on both surfaces of a hollow cylinder. The increase in storage capacity was vitiated by the disastrous reduction in angular momentum. *Compare* FASTRAND.

down *adv.* [From Old Norse *dūnn* "the soft plumage of a seabird's tits," whence "a feather bed."] Moving from an upright, operational, busy, and boring posture to one of horizontal relaxation. *Compare* UP.

downtime *n.* The period during which a system is error-free and immune from user input. *Compare* UPTIME. *See also* CRASH.

DP attorney *n.* An attorney whose own law firm has not yet computerized, and who is therefore able to exude a proper and expensive objectivity when faced with the tiresome loops of litigation between user and manufacturer.

♦Until juries are selected by technical rather than common-sense qualifications, a heavy burden rests on the attorneys involved in complex DP actions. There is little point in the aspiring Perry Mason yelling at the jury: "This so-called programmer, cowering in the dock behind a patently false beard, would have you believe that, on the night of the 25th, when all the operators were in the rest rooms and he alone was at the console, that my client's widely respected operating system suddenly and without premeditation killed Job 148, a harmless FORTRAN background batch routine which had been idly ticking over for 18 hours at least. Need I remind you, sweet members, that Job 148 has run regularly each week for 15 years, taking, typically, 19.6 hours with no observable degradation of the timesharing service? Exhibits 23 through 7856, showing the relevant operator logsheets since September 1965, can leave you in no doubt about this. The plaintiff's absurd counter that the log for December 24, 1970, is missing is a despicable red herring underlining the poverty of his submission. Why, then, I pray, would Job 148 on this fateful night be aborted by the system? You have no doubt studied Exhibits 1 through 5, the basic documentation of my client's os. In any of the nine hundred pages, I ask, is there the remotest sign of instability, the merest suspicion of nonresolvable conflict between batch and timesharing resource allocation? Who had the most to gain from the untimely demise of Job 148? I direct your attention, members of the jury, to exhibits 7857 through 12,345, the actual, unarguable hexdump printouts which the plaintiff tried to shred on the morning of the 26th. The shredder would not swallow such infamy, and neither will this court! Observe the 29765A34F in column 5 of page 3451. The most innumerate of plaintiffs could not deny the damning significance of this. This, I submit, is the smoking revolver, the flagrante delicto, the reason the accused is now attempting to escape via the window behind the dock. Yes, *he* killed Job 148! *He* wanted to load the 60K SNOBOL compiler. Our case rests, Your Honor. Forgive me if I feel and appear a little Godlike; a touch of the Ellery Queens. I must go now and prepare my invoice."

DP dictionary *n. Also called* **DP glossary.** An attempt to freeze the volatile vocabulary of an illiterate industry. This work is the first such to succeed.

DP fraud *n.* 1 The supplier's 300 percent markup. 2 The user's refusal to pay because of petty contractual quibbles, such as nondelivery, nonperformance, force mineure, and bankruptcy. 3 *(Rare)* An individual's failure to report unexpected bank credits or undercalculated invoices.

DP litigation *n. Chiefly* the IBM–Justice Department antitrust action.

▶The few DP ATTORNEYS not engaged in this legal marathon usually act on behalf of one or more of IBM's bickering rivals. Minimum punitive damages of $1 billion are regularly claimed from IBM (but never received) on the grounds that IBM's successful and profitable policy of keeping most of their customers happy constitutes unfair competition and restraint of trade. Other areas of DP litigation which arise from time to time include the vexing problem of copyright. One defendant, accused of copying a general ledger package, received the following solomonic judgment: "The jury has, quite correctly in my view, found you guilty, and my first reaction was to grant you the maximum sentence permitted under the 1980 Protection of Packages (Whether Operational or Not) Act, namely 10 years confined to your present terminal with no upgrade options. On further, more merciful reflection, it being but your sixth offense this year, it occurred to both the plaintiff and this judgeship that your unique ability to duplicate diskettes using COPFLOP level 3.4 and FLOPCOP level 4.3 on the plaintiff's system arouses such a heady mix of curiosity, admiration, and disbelief that the more appropriate punishment, subject to your approval, ultra vires and nolo contendere, would be an immediate and indefinite promotion to DPM at the plaintiff's site, full costs in this matter, and an irrevocable undertaking on your part to devote your undoubted talents to the greed of the plaintiff rather than to your own. The court be now upstanding until the Friday forenoon following the next St. Presper's Day."

The 1980 act (op. cit.) was carefully drafted to prevent countersuits from those who illegally copied inefficient or bug-ridden software. The notorious sequence of English cases *(Bloggs* v. *Lloyds; Bloggs* v. *Rex,* and *Bloggs* v. *Regina)* stretching from 1940 to 1972 clearly influenced the law remakers. As is now widely known, an admitted safe cracker, Lord "Pete Blower" Bloggs, damaged his heavily insured fingertips while attempting to test the security of a Lloyds Bank deposit box outside the normal business hours of the Park Lane branch, London, England, as 1939 was staggering to an indifferent conclusion. Bloggs' counsel argued persuasively that while the normally expected combinatorial defenses were perfectly "valeat quantum valere potest," the bona fide "furunculus armariolorum" (innocent tester of small safes) should not also have to cope with dangerously burred edges on the coded knobs. Lloyds had clearly violated the Office Appliance Safety Ordinances of 1896 and the many amendments thereto (1901–1948). Further, the plaintiff had failed to secure any financial compensation from his "actus non facit reum, nisi mens est rea." The plaintiff's injury and wrongful incarceration had deprived the plaintiff and the plaintiff's backers of proven recidivist income. "While the plaintiff is unable to engage in his trade," urged counsel, "employing skills to which we all have contributed, Society itself is in the dock." Counsel then joined the jury in a spirited rendition of:

> The banks are made of marble
> With a guard at every door;
> And the vaults are stuffed with silver
> That Lord Bloggs sweated for!

"The Banks of Marble"*—Les Rice

Less dramatic but equally relevant actions have followed. Burglars, slipping as they benchmarked suburban hallways in full pursuit of their vocational expectations, have successfully sued not only the hallway owner, but also the Shiny Wax Corporation. Correcting these anomalies, the 1980 Package Protection Act can be summed up as "Caveat Fur" (let the thief beware!), or, to paraphrase Iago, "Who copies my file, steals trash."—*Othello.*

DPM *n.* [Diplomatic Psychiatric Mediator *or* Demented Programmer Minder. *Rare* Data Processing Manager.]

◆In a typical medium-sized commercial installation, the DPM ensures that the payroll runs on time, that the month-to-date errors are cleared each month, and that the quarter-to-date errors are cleared each quarter. Typically, the DPM becomes a free agent before the year-to-date discrepancies ruin the office Christmas party.

DP VOGUE *n.* A daily glossy magazine devoted to the transitory topics of computer science. Originally modeled on the eponymous sartorial monthly, it soon required a higher publicational frequency to cope with the swings and arrows of fashionable computing.

dump *n. & v.intrans.* [Origin: English *dump* "a dull, gloomy state of mind, low spirits; a thick, ill-shaped lump or hunk of anything; to deposit something in a heap or unshaped mass, as from a cart."] **1** *n., also called* **postmortem dump.** The bewildered, numerical mapping of each molecule of a corpse in order to establish the cause of death. The excessive volume of evidence is self-defeating, insofar as putrefaction outpaces analysis. **2** *v.intrans.* To test the "0" and "1" printer or display elements at random intervals. More advanced dumps may also exercise the "2" through "7" printer capabilities, while state-of-the-art dumps provide tests for some of the alphabetic characters.

◆Dumps *are* rather depressing, but looking on the bright side, they provide an excellent check on the paper-low warning device.

dynamic *adj.* **1** (Of a RAM) in need of constant refreshment. **2** (Of a dump) unexpected, unwelcome. **3** (Of a young executive) despised, short-lived. **4** (Of an IBM System/370 model 155, 165 Address Translator) expensive.

dynamic halt *n.* *Also called* **loop halt, loop stop.** The name given, retrospectively, to an endless loop discovered in MY PROGRAM.

dyslexia *n.* [Greek *dys-* "with difficulty, abnormal" + *lexia* "reading."] A disease pandemic among cheap input peripherals, wealthy illiterates, and prrofredders.

dyxlesia *n.* The self-diagnosis of a dyslectic. *See* DYSLEXIA.

E13B *n.*   A font designed for Madison Avenue and check sorters at the expense of human legibility.

EBCDIC *n.* \Pronounced *ebb-see-dick.* \ [Acronym for Extended Binary-Coded Decimal Interchange Code.]   An 8-bit code devised for the IBM System/360 and based on the earlier 12-bit IBM card code. *Compare* ASCII.

▶Initial objections from the Jacquard Automatic Weaving Syndicate (JAWS) were quickly silenced by the allocation of codes for CC (Change Color), EW (End Woof), TWE (Time Warp Escape), SLCSM (Switch to Low-Cost String Manipulation), and FB (Fairisle Begin).

editor *n.*   A software product capable of generating copies of a program or text with random variations.

▶These variations usually arise from spurious mutations generated by the editor itself, but sometimes the user is allowed to collate his or her own random strings, known as *corrections.* If the *edited* copy is usefully near to the original, it is called a VERSION; otherwise, it is referred to as a BACKUP. *See also* TEXT EDITOR.

electron *n.*   [Origin: eponymous heroine of the Greek novel *Forever Amber.*]   The smallest and most mobile of the charged elementary particles.

▶Luckily for the industry named after her, the electron is also the most enduring, in spite of her driving habits. She consistently ignores the road signs on circuit diagrams and drives on the right against the arrows, from output to input, flagrantly violating the clearly marked potential gradients. *See also* LOGICAL DIAGRAM.

Else, Dangling   *See* DANGLING ELSE.

emulation *n.* [Latin *emulgēre* "to drain out, exhaust."] A pack of hardware and software tricks dealt by the manufacturer, allowing the user to acquire a more expensive replacement system without the attendant miseries, or improvements, of an UPGRADE. *See also* LIBERATION; SIDEGRADE.

▶The main commercial advantage of the generality of the general-purpose computer is that machine *A* can be so programmed and interfaced that the user encounters patterns of error and delay normally associated with machine *B*. Indeed, if the emulation is extended to repainting the cabinets and falsifying the invoice letterhead, the user may well remain unaware of the switch. Emulating slow, sequential processors on fast, parallel systems (while retaining all the idiosyncrasies of card-based batchness and parlaying years of RPG effort) has proved so successful that one wonders why, for example, there are still IBM 1400 installations not yet sidegraded to the 360/370 elysium. Current, and more challenging, research centers on the problem of emulating large-scale efficient mainframe systems on tiny, inefficient MICROPROCESSORS.

endless loop *n.* *See* LOOP, ENDLESS.

▶In YOUR PROGRAM, an endless loop is known as an *elementary blunder,* whereas in MY PROGRAM it is called a DYNAMIC HALT. See the accompanying illustration.

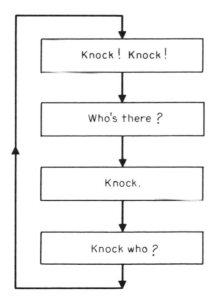

end user *n.* [Origin: from *end* "the point in time at which something ceases, termination of existence, death, fragment, remnant," + USER.] A user forced to accept the fact that the blissful days awaiting delivery will never return. *See also* REALITY.

English *n.* [© Microdata Corporation.] **1** The least unnatural of the natural languages, likely to spread from Boston to other parts of the United States. **2** A programming language supported by the Logical Machine Corporation's ADAM, and the Microdata Corporation REALITY systems. "Do not adjust your terminal, there is a fault with Reality."

◆The Reality programmer's guide includes the complete *Oxford English Dictionary,* ample proof of their claim that it offers the most exhausting documentation.

environment *n.* One of many phatic circumlocutions originating in the DP environment which has now spread to other environments.

TABLE OF ENVIRONMENTS*

In the office	In an office environment†
On the moon	In a lunar environment
In vacuo	In an empty environment
At home	In an in-house environment
Under DOS	In a DOS environment
	or
	Under a DOS environment
Crashed	In the nonfunctioning environment
Chaotic	In an unstructured environment

*Note the common shift from the definite to the indefinite article.

†Since weight and weightiness are highly regarded in DP documentation, the right-hand column variations should be used on all occasions.

Note: From the San Francisco *Examiner/Chronicle,* Sunday, November 9, 1980:

> During the sentencing, judge Stanley Frosh said Melton needed a more structured environment, such as a pre-release camp. It was then that Melton reached into his pocket and swallowed the poison, calmly washing it down with a glass of water, witnesses said. His wife, after fondly patting her husband, swallowed the white powder before a deputy could stop her.

Moral: The phrase "structured environment" should be avoided.

EPSS *n.* Abbreviation for EXPERIMENTAL PACKAGE SWITCHING SYSTEM.

Ethelred OS *n.* An operating system aimed at the ongoing nonuser environment. *See* SUPERCOMPUTER.

◆Non-ICL users, as opposed to ICL nonusers, will need reminding that when the British company International Computers Limited launched its 1900 series in 1959, it was faced with two minor embarrassments. First, there were predictable sniggers, fostered by the competition, that 1900 was the design vintage. These jokes, in fact, backfired, since the average English prospect reckoned that 1900 was *a very good year,* suggesting systems of imperious, Victorian stability, in contrast to the ghastly frog-plagued times evoked by a Univac 1108, or the futuristic uncertainties of a CDC 6400. Second, ICL had embarked on a sequence of reignwise-refined operating systems called George I, George II, . . . while a breathless, indifferent, historically confused market checked the diverse merits of the Hanoverian succession. Would George III madly relinquish the American market? The Ethelred OS was introduced at this point to initiate a new, more honest, regal software genealogy.

EWOM *n.* [Acronym for Erasable Write-Only Memory. © Irish Business Machines.] A refinement of the WOM (Write-Only Memory) allowing the chip to be erased by (1) a fresh write sequence, (2) exposure to infrared light, (3) in-depth frying for 2 hours with a portion of rock salmon, (4) a stick of gelignite.

exception reporting *n.* A system with intermittent printer problems.

exit *v. intrans.* To attempt to leave the current program by typing a sequence of ignored farewells. *See also* HALTING PROBLEM.

◆Many interactive systems shyly resist invocation, but once invoked, stubbornly refuse to step down at the user's request. If the mandatory signing-off slogan is not immediately available or effective, try a harmless prime number sieve, and await the machine's natural rejection. *See* MTBF.
There is, as yet, no standard string for use in the discontinuant environment. Contenders under urgent review include **BYE, PISS OFF, END, ADIEU, BREAK, PARTING IS SUCH SWEET SORROW,** and the ASCII standard 14-pound hammer aimed at the screen (or two such hammers for the "control + C" interrupt option). LISP (*see* table at ACRONYM) addicts will need to surround their Abschied or Hammerschaft with a reasonable number of brackets.

Experimental Package Switching System *n. Also called* EPSS. An ongoing, potentially never-ending project dedicated to ensuring the consistent misdirection of long messages in large communications networks.

▶The misrouting of stringent strings, e.g., telegraphic platitudes of five words or less, even under the primitive protocols of Morse, Baudot, and Don Ameche, can be achieved with the minimum of effort, and is subject to the Shannon-Heisenberg uncertainty principle, "If the *content* of a message is 'fixed,' there is an unavoidable error in determining its *destination*, and vice versa." This delicate balance between message mutilation and misdirection seems to break down with strings of higher DENIER and increased signaling rates. Attempts to introduce new conceptual invariants, such as the *charm* of the longer message, were vitiated by recent ALLC experiments in which the entire text of *Gone with the Wind* was injected into the ARPA network. The message emerged, with less than the predicted number of stylistic aberrations, on the TRS-80 cassette library of X. P. Qume in Ottumwa, Iowa. It appears that the extra momentum of heavy, fast-moving messages overcomes the intended switching strategy at certain nodes, rather as a runaway locomotive jumps the points.

Extended BASIC *n.* [From *extended* "fully stretched, prolonged" + BASIC.]   Any BASIC compiler or interpreter enhanced with features stolen from COBOL and meeting any two of the following conditions: (1) the cost exceeds $40.00, (2) line numbers can be incremented automatically or omitted, (3) tape cassettes are not supported.

FASTRAND *n.* [© Sperry Rand Corporation.]   A nonfloppy rotating cylindrical device used for storing angular momentum.

▶In the event of power failure, the FASTRAND can be coupled to a standby generator for several days. Note that the total angular momentum available is slightly reduced if the data-storage option is fitted, owing to the braking effect of the read-write heads on the magnetized drum surface. Three or more FASTRANDs should not be switched on simultaneously at the same site without consulting Sperry's in-house geophysicist. The latter will also advise on the correct latitude-dependent orientation of the drum axis to avoid data loss due to coriolis forces.

FIFO *adj.* [Acronym for First In, First Out.]   (Of a STACK) Able to "deal from the bottom," using legerdestack. *Compare* LIFO; *see also* LINO in table at ACRONYM.

finite-state *adj.*   **1** (Of a sales tax) ranging from 0 to 100 percent, depending on the state.   **2** (Of a machine) having a limited repertoire.

▶It can be proved that if a finite-state machine is left to run long enough —for 24 hours prior to a payroll deadline, say—at least one machine state will recur. This is known as the *error state*. See also TURING MACHINE; UTM.

firmware *n.*   A neutral, noware zone between hardware and software, free to deflect blame in either direction, and enabling problems to be solved by three sets of modifications rather than one.

first-time *adj.*   (Of a user) virginal and secretly panting for the salesperson's sacrificial knife.

▶A few first-time users somehow survive the bloody initiation:

"I didn't like it the first time,
But, Oh! how it grew on me."

"The Spinach Song"—Julie Lee

fix *n. & v.trans.* [Latin *figĕre* "to attack with reproaches, to render immovable."] **1** *n.* A palliative shot in the system's arm, becoming less effective with each application. **2** *v.trans.* To remove (a BUG) by redefining the program specification in order to take advantage of an unexpected feature. *See also* DEBUGGING.

fleep *n. Also called* **feep, bleep, beep.** [From JARGON FILE.] The soft bell sound emitted by a display terminal.

◆The softness of the fleep varies according to the VDU and the calamity signaled. The fleep of the VT-52 has been compared to the sound of a '52 Chevy stripping its gears.

flip-flop *n.* **1** A primitive and noisy bistable device.

◆ Flip; flip flop;
The circuit keeps a squeggin'
And it won't stop;
Flip; flip flop;
I guess I'll have to change it
To a good Kipp;
What is it, it does to me?
What mad kind of thrill do I find?
Switchin' on the **HT,** the **LT:**
Don't know it's alive but
It's driving me out of my . . .
Flip; flip flop;
The circuit keeps a squeggin'
And it just won't stop . . . flip flop!

2 A double-sided FLOPPETTE.

◆As in the pop record industry, the more popular tracks are usually stored on the *flip* side.

floppette *n. Also called* **floppy disk, diskette.** [Diminutive of *flop* "failure."] Any of various nonhard memory devices with nonsoft error propensities. *See also* FLIP-FLOP; FLOPPY DRUM.

◆Floppettes must be handled with great care. Keep away from tobacco smoke, grease, nuclear reactors, gravitional fields, ballpoint pens, fingers, meteorites, untreated sewage, and floppy-disk drives. Always store away from strong moonlight at 0 kelvin in a neutrino-free environment. Before discarding used, that is, encoded, floppettes, read Irish Business Machines' racy leaflet *1001 Things To Do with Old Floppettes.* Table mats, coasters, flower-pot drainers, and models of the Taj Mahal are among the many bright gift ideas.

floppy drum *n.* [© Irish Business Machines.] An early low-cost mass memory device, now superseded by the FLOPPETTE.

▶Conversion from floppy drum to disk is not difficult, and can be undertaken by any user of average intelligence using everyday household tools. Simply cut along the dotted line and reshape as required. (See the accompanying illustration.) IBM provide free 5- and 8-inch templates. Simply send the crate tops from three 370/168 systems plus $1.98 for postage, packing, and insurance.

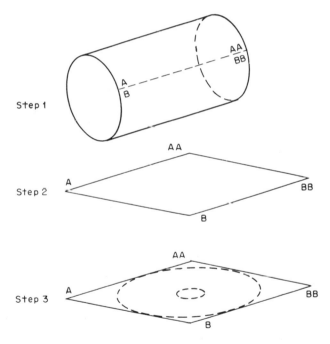

flowchart *n. & v.* [From *flow* "to ripple down in rich profusion, as hair" + *chart* "a cryptic hidden-treasure map designed to mislead the uninitiated."] **1** *n.* The solution, if any, to a class of Mascheroni construction problems in which given algorithms require geometrical representation using only the 35 basic ideograms of the ANSI template. **2** *n.* Neronic doodling while the system burns. **3** *n.* A low-cost substitute for wallpaper. **4** *n.* The innumerate misleading the illiterate. "A thousand pictures is worth ten lines of code."—*The Programmer's Little Red Vade Mecum,* Mao Tse T'umps, Subversive Software Publications, 1968. **5** *n.* A set of systems analysts' Rausch tests, revealing their innermost, twisted procedural fantasies. (See the accompanying illustration.) **6** *v.intrans.* To produce flowcharts with no particular object in mind. **7** *v.trans.* To obfuscate (a problem) with esoteric cartoons.

Algorithm for maximizing human happiness

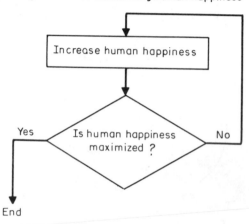

foolproof *adj.* (Of a system) inaccessible by the USER.

foot worm *n.* *Also called* **ring worm.** A graduate INCH WORM who, forsaking marigolds, mensurates on the branches of labeled trees.

FORTRAN *n.* [Acronym for FORmula TRANslating system.] One of the earliest languages of any real height, level-wise, developed out of Speedcoding by Backus and Ziller for the IBM/704 in the mid-1950s in order to boost the sales of 80-column cards to engineers.

◗In spite of regular improvements (including a recent option called STRUCTURE), it remains popular among engineers but despised elsewhere. Many rivals, with the benefit of hindsight, have crossed swords with the old workhorse! Yet FORTRAN gallops on, warts and all, more transportable than syphilis, fired by a bottomless pit of working subprograms. Lacking the compact power of APL, the intellectually satisfying elegance of ALGOL

68, the didactic incision of Pascal, and the spurned universality of PL/1, FORTRAN survives, nay, flourishes, thanks to a superior investmental inertia.

freelance *adj.* [Origin: either *free* "expensive" (as, "the best things in life are free") + *lance* "a large lancelet, a not-so-diminutive fishlike animal," or from 15th-century weapons sales jingle: "Buy three lances, get one free!"] Immune from litigation.

FS *n.* [Future Series. © IBM.] *Also called* **Freundliches Schwert (Friendly Sword).** [© Richard Wagner] A sword of Damocles for the non-IBM minority.

▶IBM's next product announcement, or possibly the one after the next. Who knows if the FS is really hanging over the marketplace? IBM's announcement that "FS is suspended" is ambiguous, to say the least. Cynics say that FS will be a 1401 for $20 (printer ribbons and software not included); others say it will be level 3 of ACF/NCP/VS or a 7090 emulator for the 4331. Myth has it that a Heldenprogrammer will one day descend on the misty Poughkeepsie Nibelheim singing "I'm busy doing Notung"; he will reforge the mighty FS, rescue Grace Brünhopper from a burning Bluebell mountaintop, and restore IBM's rightful 100 percent share of the market. For was it not written:

Da hast du die Stücken,	(Well, there are the bits,
schändlicher Stümper	You blundering botcher!
. . . .	. . . .
Warst du entzwei	You were unstable
ich zwang dich zu ganz;	But I have made you whole;
kein Schlag soll nun dich mehr	You are now completely
zerschlagen	user-proof.)

—Act I, *Siegfried,* Richard Wagner.

function *n.* A device for mapping a domain of unknown ARGU-MENTS onto a range of inaccessible results.

gangpunch *v.trans.* To ensure that a sequence of cards is mispunched consistently.

gate *n.* One of the nine Apollinarian "portes" to algorasmic bliss.

gee whiz *adj.* Relating to some superficially flashy aspect of technology intended to amuse and distract the layperson.

general-purpose graphs *n.* [© Irish Business Machines.] A set of graphical visual aids designed to reduce your overhead overheads. See the illustration on pages 57 and 58.

Gershwin's law It ain't necessarily so.

GIGO *n.* Acronym for Gospel In, Garbage Out.

gilding the lily *n.* The fruitless attempt to improve an already perfect system, e.g., by replacing a data cassette with a floppy disk, or by "upgrading" from a 360 to a 370.

glass tty *n.* *pronounced* glass titty.\\ [From JARGON FILE.] A CRT terminal so lacking in features that it behaves like a TTY.

glitch *n. & v.trans.* [Origin: possibly blend of *glitter* + *hitch* or Yiddish *glitsh-'n* "slip, skid."] **1** *n.* Any unexpected and transient fluctuation in the power supply or, by extension, any sudden change for the worse in the status quo. **2** *v.trans.* To upset (a component or system) by the, usually unintentional, addition of a glitch. **3** *v.trans.* (*See* JARGON FILE: local usage, Stanford University, California.) To engage in SCROLLING (on a display screen). *See also* GRITCH.

global *adj.* [Latin *globus* "a ball."] **1** (Of a variable) able to bounce around the system, transferring arbitrary values to and from unconnected programs. **2** (Of an error) ideal; detectable; correctable; minor. *Compare* LOCAL.

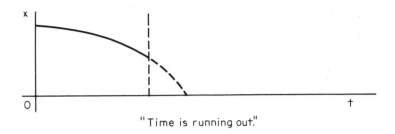

"Time is running out."

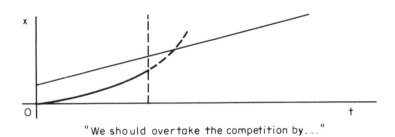

"We should overtake the competition by..."

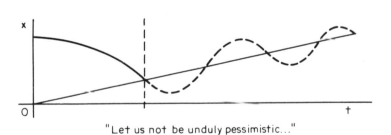

"Let us not be unduly pessimistic..."

"We have maintained our traditional marketing
supremacy in the Southwest."

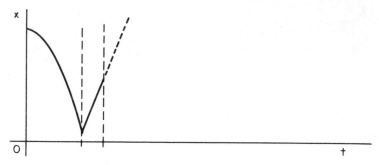

"Your new Board of Directors is confident that..."

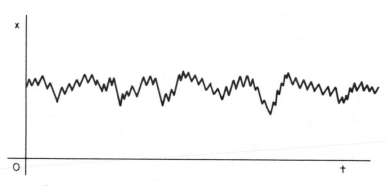

"In the absence of any clear trends we are holding the
dividend at..."

▶All unavoidable errors should be made global. Local errors can lurk around unnoticed for months, gathering malignant momentum, suppurating behind the scenes until the system suddenly collapses from the sheer mass of smegmous accretion. *See* SOFTWARE ROT.

GOD *n.*   Acronym for **General Oracle Dispenser**. *See* SUPERCOMPUTER.

Godot *n.*   A sarcastic name applied generally to any project or device which fails to materialize after the *n*th deadline.

golf ball *n.*   A spherical printing device, so called from its early propensity to fly off in random directions to unpredictable places.

▶An Olivetti model (serial #098-43245) holds the world record for distance: 546 yards at St. Andrews University, Scotland, on January 3, 1969, using a specially dimpled character set. M. Thumps holds the record for the most golf balls lost during a single round of on-line editing. In a 12-hour session at the IBM Selectric British Rail TRAIN system terminal (*see* CURSOR), Thumps lost 89 golf balls (comprising 16 distinct typefaces). During this period, incidentally, he also lost five trains, three friends, a $500 productivity bonus, and his job.

A hole in one has been claimed by Ann Arbor University, Michigan, but the details are too disgusting to merit objective reportage.

gosub *n.* [From verb "go" and Latin *sub* "under."] A CALL made on some nonexistent or noncooperative routine, resulting in instant downage.

goto *n. & v. & adj.* **1** *n.* A GOTO ORDER. **2** *v.trans.* To transfer control (to a distant line or label). **3** *v.intrans.* To transfer control to nowhere in particular. **4** *adj.* (Of an order or instruction) hazardous, irresponsible, fatal, inviting contempt.

goto order *n.* [Origin: possibly Biblical: "Go to, let us go down and confound their language."—Jehovah at Babel (*Genesis* 11:7); or possible metathesis of "order *to go,*" (U.S.) term used in the cafeteria system.] A delightful but dangerous feature of many primitive (unstructured) mid-level languages, whereby a programmer can pass control to some remote, unwritten part of a program and break for coffee. *Compare* COME FROM.

◗The powerful academic lobby promoting GOTOless programming [e.g., al-Khāsī (1449), Dijkstra (1968), Wirth (1970), and Knuth (1970)] received support from an unexpected direction when Anthony Newley's recording of *Where Shall I Goto?* made the charts in 1976.

grandfather-father-son *adj.* Being or pertaining to three files believed to have some genealogical relationship. Owing to the hazards of updating and genetic mutation (*see* SOFTWARE ROT), the grandfather, if still alive, carries more authority.

◗Those who seek some neo-Darwinian interpretation of the evolution of programs and data files are thwarted by the complexities of ONE-LINE PATCHes, the conflicting definitions of fitness and survival, the apparent death wish of DPMs, and the morphogenetic instability of the editing process. "For the sins of Mk I shall visit Ye, yea unto the *N*th generation." —St. Presper's *Stridor Dentium,* Incisor IV, molar iii.

graphics *n. Also called* **graphical display systems; graphical plotting systems.** Any system capable of, and mainly engaged in, the display or printing of continuous-line Snoopy renditions.

great moments in computing history *n.* A collection of boring anecdotes: as,

> "Paging Mr. Samas, paging Mr. Samas. . . . There's a Mr. Powers on the line. . . ."

> "Professor Wilkes, the man's here with the mercury. . . ."

> "T. J., I think we should call it *virtual memory.* . . ."

> "Yes, I know it's small, but we can still use the big cabinets. . . ."

> "But, Grace, darling, that will allow *anyone* to program. . . ."

gritch *n. & v.* [Origin: possibly exclamation "Grrr" + "hitch" or corruption of GLITCH.] **1** *n.* A complaint or expression of frustration (usually following a glitch). **2** *v.intrans.* To complain. **3** *v.trans.* To GLITCH (a component or system).

Grosch's law [Formulated by Herbert R. J. Grosch in the late 1940s.] "Computing power is proportional to the square of system cost."

▶K. E. Knight has shown that up to 1976, in spite of diverse changes in technology, leasing policies, and inflation, Grosch's law had been religiously observed by the costing and marketing departments of the major DP manufacturers. "And so it was done that the Grosch prophet be maintained."—St. Presper's *Admonishments to the Parasites* (Level III, release iv). To some, the mini and micro revolutions have obscured the validity of Grosch's law, but it remains honored in the canon of mainframe orthodoxy. Indeed, cynics in the latter camp point out that the equation

$$P = kC^2$$

where P = computing power, C = cost, and k is the Grosch constant of proportionality, is vacuously true for mini- and microcomputers, with $P = k = 0$ for all values of C. The nonabashed mainframer still dreams of exploiting Grosch's law by buying bigger and costlier systems, and sections of the industry will forever try to oblige. *See* GROSCH'S LAW, COROLLARY TO; SUPERCOMPUTER.

Grosch's law, corollary to "Development cost is proportional to the cube of the target performance." *See also* GROSCH'S LAW; SUPERCOMPUTER.

grunge *n.* [Origin obscure: possibly onomatopoeic blend of *grunt* and *cringe.*] The patina which eventually enhances all hardware and software exposed to the human environment.

▶A janitorian writes: "A really healthy grunge takes time and should not be rushed. Smegmologists worth their salt can sniff out an artificially accelerated layer of grunge with instant disdain. Genuine grunge is not only an object of sublime beauty, a palimpsest of DP endeavor, but also a threatened source of information to the industrial microarcheologist. Many installations, despite regular upgrades, retain some vestigial reminders of earlier, happier days—a bypassed accounting machine, a 90-column sorter, perhaps, or a sales analysis written in RPG-1—either for sentimental reasons or from sheer necessity. Patient probing of the grungial strata residing on these bygones can reveal unexpected facts about earlier DP cultures. Our present knowledge, however scanty, of the Collator People, for example, stems entirely from microdigs made in the 1970s at MIT, a site still rated highly by grunge sifters and DP historians. The janitorian fellowship is united in its effort to avoid the mindless removal of vital evidence from computer equipment. As Dr. Thumpton, the doyen of DP microarcheology, once explained, 'Each console fingermark, each keyboard coffee stain, each half-removed adhesive label is a priceless, sacred token of our heritage.' "

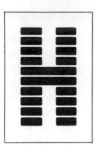

hair *n.*   The subsumed substance that makes problems, programs, and devices HAIRY. *See also* HIRSUTE.

◗The Scouse dialect, as spoke in Liverpool and contagious suburbs, has a similar adjective-to-noun transformation. Anything which is "tatty" owes its "tattiness" to the presence of "tats."

hairy *adj.*   **1** (Of a program or system) unduly complex, overly convoluted, beyond fathomage, trichomatic. **2** (Of a person) weak-chinned, complexifying, able to add or subtract HAIR according to demand. "For I am an hairy man, but Alan was an smooth man." —*De Arte Publicā Stātūque Artis (Concerning the Art of the State and the State of the Art)*, St. Presper. *See also* DEPILATION.

Halting problem *n.*   **1** *DP* The problem of stopping a computation between crashes.

◗An engineer writes: "Users sometimes want to interrupt a job without waiting for the system to abort it. If the machine has no stop or suspend facility (or if these functions fail to work), we recommend the use of the power-off switch rather than removing the power plug. The latter action occasionally invokes a standby battery (if fitted), and your unwanted job or endless loop will continue. Even the power-off switch will not always guarantee termination because of what we engineers call the *running-on problem*. As with the analogous automotive problem, the cure is to clean all the contacts, check the timing, and try a higher-octane power supply.

2 *Computer science* The abstract problem, solved negatively by Alan M. Turing, which, essentially, seeks a general method for deciding whether any arbitrary program will terminate or not in a crashless environment.

◗Turing's formal proof of the nonexistence of the programmer's much-needed touchstone is closely related to Gödel's work on undecidable propositions. The curious laity should drop everything and read Douglas R. Hofstadter, *Gödel, Escher, Bach: An Eternal Golden Braid,* Basic Books, Inc., New York, 1979. The undercurious are referred to the accompanying illustration, which, according to DP folklore, was jotted on the back of an envelope by Turing during a London-Cambridge train journey with Strachey.

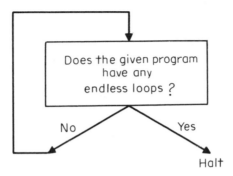

hard sector *n.*   That area of a disk being currently accessed.

hardware *n.*   The easy part of the system. *Compare* FIRMWARE; MIDDLEWARE; SOFTWARE.

◗The callosity of a *ware* is best judged by considering the difficulties faced by the goods inward clerk as incoming items are checked against the supplier's advice note. Receipts such as:

4-off Frames, boards, mother, holding, S-100, 6" bolts, retaining, hexagonal, tapping, self, aluminum. Part # 360/168-PDQ-362516526/A

present fewer problems than, say:

1-off Disk, floppy, teeny-weeny Pascal, level 56.127, contains all fixes in appendices 12-68 of attached release dated 12/10/84.

or:

1-Mbyte add-on virtual memory.

Hartree constant *n.* *Also called* **Hartree's constant.** [After Douglas Raynor Hartree (1897–1958), English physicist and computer pioneer.]   The fixed time interval H between now t and the time T_a when any given DP project is completed.

◗If T_i is the time when a promise is made to complete a project at time T_p, then

$$T_a > t \geq T_p \geq T_i$$

and

$$T_a - t = H$$

It follows that

$$\lim_{t \to \infty} T_a = \infty$$

i.e., DP projects are never completed.

Henny Thumpman See King of the one-line patchers.

heuristics *n.* 1 The art of looking busy when seated at a terminal. 2 An upmarket problem-solving methodology still seeking a worthy class of problems.

hexadecimal *adj.* *Also called* **hexadismal.** [Greek *hexe* "witch," whence "evil spell" + Latin *decem* "ten."] Relating to a much-cursed method of alpha-numerological counting, whereby two spiders can be dissected for the hell-broth cauldron. Cordon Bleu hags intone 0 through 9 as they toss in the first ten tarantulid tarsi; the remaining six stumps carry the mnemonical incantation A through F: "Azazel, Beelzebub, Cacodemon, Diablo, Eblis, Fiend."

◗Current DP usage retains the demonic, hexadecimal notation 0 to 9, A to F for the bit patterns 0000 to 1111, but William Barden, Jr. (*TRS-80 Assembly Language Programming,* Radio Shack, 1979) has updated the mnemonic to: "Actinium, Barium, Curium, Dysprosium, Erbium, Fernium."

high-level language *n.* 1 Any of a set of acronyms devised by the manufacturer's marketing division. 2 A natural language purged of ambiguity *and* semantics, but with compensatory punctuational and diacritical extensions aimed at increasing the complexity of the syntactical structure. 3 A method of slowing down the system to allow the innumerate to cope.

hirsute *adj.* Humorously endowed with a pleonasm of plethoric profundity, i.e., HAIR.

hole *n.* 1 The space in a medium formerly occupied by a CHAD. 2 The resulting region of a Babbage wooden memory board when a knot-hole is reset. *See also* NOT-; PUNCH.

however *conj.* A disjunctive used to separate the assertion of a proposition and the immediate assertion of its negation: "We plan to go live tomorrow; however, the multiply subroutine still leaves much to be desired." "We accept your quotation and performance estimates; however, we await the results of the benchmark promised last June."

IBM *n.* [International Business Machines Corporation.] *Also called* **Itty Bitty Machines, Snow White, The VS Pioneer, The Lawyer's Friend.** The dominant force in computer marketing, having, worldwide, supplied some 75 percent of all known hardware and 10 percent of all known software. To protect itself from the litigious envy of less successful organizations, such as the U.S. government, IBM employs 68 percent of all known ex-attorneys general.

▶An IBM watcher writes: "I am often asked to explain IBM's leading position in data processing. My reply, in a word, *infallibility.* No cheap tricks or gimmicks. No loss-making innovations. Just honest-to-goodness, expensive *infallibility.* If IBM's rivals—formerly called the Seven Dwarfs, with Univac as Doc and Telex as Grumpy, but now more accurately referred to as the Seven Hundred Midgets—would only eschew their fruitless, vindictive crusades against the one, true, everlasting orthodoxy and attend to their own blatant fallibilities, we would see fewer fatalities in the DP marketplace." *See also* ABM; FS; THINK SIGN.

ICARUS *n.* [Acronym for Infallible, Comprehensive, And Running User Software.] A software house which aimed too high and was mortally singed.

▶The staff made redundant by the ICARUS dive have both forsaken the cruel world of computing and are now working for ICL.

Ideal Business Machine *n.* A sublime, cost-no-object **VTMI** (Very Total Management Information) system being developed for the 1984 Meanman-Narkus personal computer catalog.

▶The architecture is the joint responsibility of von Neumann and Turing assisted by Wilkes, Eckert, Mauchly, Hartree, Cray, Amdahl, Babbage, Williams, and Pascal, based on components supplied by English Eclectic. The systems and applications software team includes Gill, Knuth, Strachey, Wirth, McCarthy, Dijkstra, Newell, Simon, Minsky, Wheeler, Arbib, Popplestone, Winograd, van Wijngaarden, Backus, Naur, Kleene, Łukasiewicz, Landin, Hoare, Floyd, Chomsky, Scott, Park, Peterson, Michaelson, Michie, Tarski, me, and Shannon. Project Director is Lord Flowers, helped by Oppenheimer, Hartley, Goldstine, and Wotan. Russell, Whitehead, Wittgenstein, and Dylan Thomas are handling the documentation (a much-needed blend of wit, fantasy, and precision). T. J. Watson, Sr., Billy Graham, and Geoff Cross are running the marketing division, while N. Bonaparte heads up field service. Site preparation is in the capable and experienced hands of G. Khan, Capability Brown, and A. Le Nôtre. Fully comprehensive, bundled, and infallible packages have been ordained in ALGOL 84 by our shit-hot package kings, Buddha, Mahomet, and Christ (proprietary rights fully protected). The other two major high-level languages, EV-LISP and EVQ-LISP, by the way, are also supported. Initial master file data will be keyed in by K. Marx and verified by F. Engels. A real Meanman-Narkus coup has been the signing of A. Einstein and H. Poincaré to oversee the file-maintenance group (any three of the nine muses, according to availability). The day-to-day data-entry team has been recruited from the Dallas Cowboy Cheerleaders, trained by Minerva, and supervised by Pope John Paul II and the Ayatollah Ruhollah Khomeini. An all-Greek squad of factory-trained operators will be provided, comprising of (sic) Plato, Socrates, Aristotle, *more,* under the watchful eye of JCL whiz-kid Zeus. On-line prognostics are guaranteed by the Delphic Service Center.

The total up-and-running ballpark end-user price has not yet been announced, but is likely to be high. But when was the *best* ever cheap? Also, some slippage timewise has been mooted. But when was the *best* not worth waiting for, indefinitely if need be?

IMP *n.* [Acronym for Integrated Morticians Package. ©ICARUS.]   A comprehensive, heart-warming package which has literally buried the competition after prolonged, in-depth trials at the Lombard Happy-Landing Chapel of Sweet Repose, Gardena, California.

▶The IMP package is a real eye-opener, and a lesson to less lively vertical markets in the proper exploitation of such modern DP techniques as postmortem dumps and decompilers. We quote from the ICARUS brochure *Stretching Your Bereavement Processing Dollar* (1979 edition):

> The IMP package is written in racy, uncontroversial MIDTRAN: ("For He shall choose between the QUIKTRAN and the DEADTRAN."— St. Presper, *Epistolatory Update to the Algolites,* level IX, release viii)

IMP's truly revelationary documentation will take you painlessly, step by joyous step, through the once-irksome cycle of bereavement processing.

Say *goodbye* to digging holes and punching cards!
Shout *farewell* to unsightly chadim on your vestments!
Scream *adieu* to clay on your boots!
Yell *no-more* to unjustified memorial epigraphy!

IMP offers the LOT! IMP prepares the LOT! IMP consecrates the LOT!
Check out the advantages!

Only IMP gives you:

Full pre- and post-need casket accounting
On-line floral tributation
Next-of-kin mailing shots
Obituarial word processing
Probate litigation (normal or noncontigency)
Will validation
Realtime corpse count
Interment logistics and plot plotting
Armband inventory control
Nondestructive crematorial temperature gradients
Automatic tombstone engraving (choice of 15 Gothic fonts)
Jazz bands (New Orleans branch only)
Firecrackers (optional)
Hertz Rent-a-Hearse network
Pre-need enrollment and training
Cosmetics (departed *and* departee)
Cryogenics
Hymn selection menus
Creative condolences (with optional personalization)
Computer-aided design (mausolea, caskets, cuisine, etc.)
FREE repeat business voucher (valid for 3 days)
All listings/invites/invoices in tasteful HAMLET-black

PLUS PLUS PLUS . . . the real killer:

The Merry Survivor option!!!

A discreet, no-questions-asked COMPU-DATE^{TM} service offering confidential, computer-matched social introductions for the semi-inconsolable!

IMP carefully vets all post-funereal dates!

NO boring fortune hunters!
NO overrated gigolos!
NO dumb gold diggers! (unless box 47 checked)
NO racial, religious, or sexual prejudice (unless box 89 checked)

The Merry Survivor option keeps YOU, the mortician, in an ongoing, profitable situation with otherwise transitory clients.

impersonal computing *n.* Routine, run-of-the-mill commercial data processing, in which the scrawled schedules Scotch-taped to the console have not been changed for 3 years. *Compare* PERSONAL COMPUTING.

implementation *n.* The fruitless struggle by the talented and underpaid to fulfill promises made by the rich and ignorant.

inch worm *n.* One engaged in spurious quantification on a small scale.

▾ Inch worm, inch worm, measuring your marigolds,
You and your arithmetic will probably go far;
Inch worm, inch worm, measuring your marigolds,
seems to me you should stop and see
How beautiful they are.*

Compare FOOT WORM; NUMEROLATRY.

incompleteness theorem *n.* 1 *Formal systems theory* A theorem establishing the incompleteness of a certain set of axioms, as: "The second-order predicate calculus is incomplete."—K. Gödel (1931). 2 *Informal systems theory* The empirically unimpeachable fact that at least one vital element in the system will not be delivered, as: "Where's the ****ing power lead?"—M. Thumps (1976).

in-house *adj.* [Origin: "Is there a doctor in-house?"—traditional appeal to a theater audience.] Being or relating to any job which the user's staff can screw up without outside help.

insinnuendo *n.* [Origin: Malapudlianism (Scouse dialect, Liverpool, for malapropistic portmanteau) from *insinuate* + *innuendo*.] The oblique implication that a certain feature or device is available as a result of its being named in a specification, proposal, or quotation.

interface *n. & v.trans.* 1 *n.* An arbitrary line of demarcation set up in order to apportion the blame for malfunctions. 2 *v.trans.* To redesign (two working subsystems) so that they can go wrong symbiotically.

---

*"The Inch Worm" from *Hans Christian Andersen* by Frank Loesser. © 1951, 1952 Frank Music Corp. © Renewed 1979, 1980 Frank Music Corp. International Copyright Secured. All Rights Reserved. Used by Permission.

introspect *n.* A VIRTUAL prospect added to forecasts in order to placate sales management and remove the finiteness restriction from the TRAVELING SALESPERSON PROBLEM.

IO *n.* [Origin obscure: either from Greek *io!* "a shout of joy following the successful mounting of a cow," or, possibly, abbreviation for Input/Output.] The Alpha and Omega of computing, and the only two aspects thereof that the layperson understands and desires. Unfortunately, the DP professional intervenes with Beta through Psi. If Omega should be reached, the cry "IO" is raised, initiating a prolonged bacchanal.

IOU *n.* *pronounced* I owe you\\ [Input/Output Unit.] A promissory instrument that is rarely honored. *See also* IO.

irregular verbs In addition to the irregular conjugations found in Standard English (e.g., *I am, you are, he is*), DP English has generated many local deviant conjugations of interest to the sociolinguist.

TABLE OF DP IRREGULAR VERBS

I construct algorithms	
You program	
He She	uses FORTRAN

I consult	
You freelance	
He She	moonlights

I chart	
You code	
He She	runs

I'm with IBM	
You're with UNIVAC	
He's She's	with NCR

I refine
You debug

TABLE OF DP IRREGULAR VERBS *(Continued)*

He She patches They kludge	
I assemble You compile He She interprets It	
I market You sell He She peddles	
I manufacture You sell He She suffers	
I heurist You try and err He She flounders	
I interact You timeshare He She hogs	
I extrapolate You conjecture He She guesses	
I was Turing You were Turing He She Tured	

I verify

You punch

He
She joggles

I curtate

You truncate

He
She shortens

IRS *n.* [Internal Revision Service.]

▶Each year the IRS meets with AUGRATIN (Amalgamated Union of General Rewriters, Amenders, Tinkerers, and INterpolators) to determine which changes in the withholding algorithms will cause the maximum dislocation to existing PAYROLL packages. Experience has shown that it is the small, apparently insignificant variations in the taxiomatic schema that create more havoc and consultancy fees than any major recasting of the income-truncation methodology. Mooted changes are tested on the joint IRS/AUGRATIN Cray Mk. II, which holds models of over 7000 payroll implementations, and refined to maximize conversion cost.

ISAM file *n.* [Acronym for Intrinsically Slow Access Method *or* (rare) Indexed Sequential Access Method.] One of the most successful data-security systems so far devised. Information is protected from all but the most persistent, patient, and devious.

ISO *n.* [Origin: possibly Greek *iso* "equal" but now presumed acronym for International Standards Organization.] A meta-standards organization set up in 1947 in order to establish standards for the setting up of standards organizations. *See also* ANSI; ASCII.

▶Having failed in this exordial assignment, and in order to regain some credibility among the growing number of national standards bodies (for each emerging nation, it seemed, considered itself not fully emerged until it had an airline *and* a standards association), ISO directed its taxonomic skills to the creation of a standard for toilet seats, to which end a widely spaced sample of assholes was recruited and exposed to the mensurational rigors of statistical humiliation. This ongoing (in both senses of the word) project is likely to be vitiated by the arrival on earth of extraterrestrial globs with nonstandard excretive methodologies.

JANUS *n.* [Acronym for JANuary Updating Service.] *See* DECADE COUNTER.

JARGON file *n.* A computerized glossary-thesaurus of DP words maintained at SAIL (the artificially intelligent oasis on the Stanford University campus) and MIT (the Massachusetts Institute of Tautology) by Mark Crispin, Raphael Finkel, Guy L. Steele Jr., and Donald Woods, with assistance from the MIT and Stanford AI communities and Worcester Polytechnic Institution.

▶Entries from this collection are reproduced with the permission of the above-mentioned compilers.

JCL *n.* [Job Control Language.] A deliberately abstruse software barrier between the USER and the OPERATING SYSTEM, set up to prevent ordinary programmers from running their own programs.

▶As the name partly implies, JCL was devised to create jobs for otherwise displaced intellectuals, and to thwart the gloomy predictions of computer-induced unemployment made in the 1950s.

job trickle *n., also (archaic)* **job stream**. The system's attempt to match the rate of execution to the programmer's coding rate.

▶A travel agent writes: "For a busman's holiday with a difference, join us on a lazy, unguided tour of the system of your choice. Relax on a structured, fully compiled program as it meanders through endless, unfrequented IO gullies, seeps by silted JCLs, and dodges the screes of the dreaded OS. Overnight stops at selected buffers; all transfers included (*you* select the baud rate); FIFO bookings accepted now; the organizers are not responsible for dammed channels or blocked pipelines."

John Birch machine *n.* [From M. A. Arbib, 1969.] A finite-state machine in which the tape moves to the right after each computation.

K *prefix* [Kilo-.] **1** *Science* Thousandfold, as: "40K brothers/Could not, with all their quantity of love,/Make up my sum."—*Hamlet.* **2** *Finance* 2^{10}-fold, providing a hidden 2.4 percent hedge against impoverishment.

▸Computer sales proposals operate in both environments and tend to fluctuate between the two K modes without proper warning. When in doubt, you should assume the worst case, e.g., "Each additional 8K of memory will cost $1K," means you get 8000 *bits* for $1024, whereas "We offer to buy back each surplus 8K memory board for $1K" should be taken as an offer of $1000 for 8192 *words.*

king of the one-line patchers. Byname for Henny Thumpman (1906–   ), stand-up programmer and court jester for Jewish Business Machines, and enumerator of such overexposed catch strings as: "I *love* this environment"; "Take my system!"; "*That* you call a feedback?"; "But for *you,* 369.95!"; "Compatible, schcompatible, so you wanna hold up progress?"; "My wife's so dumb, she wants that syntax should increase 10 percent!"

kludge *n. & v.trans., also called* **kluge** [Yiddish *klug* "smart."] **1** *n.* The programmers' vaseline. **2** *n.* A step in a STEPWISE REFINEMENT. **3** *n.* [From JARGON FILE] Something that works for the wrong reasons. **4** *v.trans.* To evade the main issue by applying a kludge (to a problem). *See also* BUG; ONE-LINE PATCH; PTF.

KSAM file *n.* [Acronym for Key Sequential Access Method.] A place where only *key* items get lost.

label *n. & v.trans.* **1** *n. Programming* An arbitrary but often mnemonic string assigned to a line in a program to which subsequent GOTO or preceding COME FROM instructions can be referenced. Labels are mainly used to distinguish the various ENDLESS LOOPS in a program. **2** *n. Magnetic media* A physical identification up front, showing author, date, content, author's bio and previous convictions, number of undetected errors, proprietary caveats, waivers reconsequential damage, and the address of the nearest attorney. Cautious users have the foregoing both dymo'd *and* digitally encoded on the leader of the medium. **3** *v.trans.* To invoke the message "duplicate label" until a unique label has been assigned (to a program line or statement).

labor-hour *n.* *See* PERSON-HOUR.

latest version *n.* *See* VERSION, LATEST.

law *n.* Any statement in the aphoristic environment, coined to amuse and distract regardless of apodictic truth or empirical verifiability.

▶Some meta-laws escape the latter qualifications, e.g.,

Kelly's pith-poor law: "Terseness is not enough."

G. B. Shaw's golden rule: "There are no golden rules."

Following a spate of undisciplined lawmaking, ASCII established the Solon Committee in 1978 to devise guidelines for the formulation of laws and their preferred typography in two major categories:

The standard ASCII 1.75-inch diameter lapel button.

The standard ASCII 11.25-inch car bumper sticker.

The rival Hammurapi Committee, set up by ISO in 1979, has accepted the latter standard, subject to some minor revisions, but utterly rejects the antiquated ASCII button size as an unjustified curb on creativity. The ISO 5.139-cm-diameter button will probably prevail, in spite of the earnest 1.845-inch compromise proposal from the United Kingdom representative.

SEE FOLLOWING ENTRIES*

Decompiling, James Joyce's law of

Gershwin's law

Grosch's law

Grosch's law, corollary to

Murphy's law of programming

Voltaire-Candide, law of

*A database of tarnished truisms initiated by Conrad Scheiker is being maintained at the Computer Center, University of Arizona, Tuscon, Arizona, 85721 by Gregg Townsend.

leader *n.*   **1** (Of a project) the person at the front, followed blindly until a break occurs. **2** (Of a magnetic or paper tape) the piece at the front, followed blindly until a break occurs. **3** (Of a punched-card deck) the veteran, battle-hardened card placed at the front of the pack to soften the defensive jaws of the opposing card reader. *Compare* TRAILER.

▶ As me an' me marrer was readin' a tyape,
The tyape gave a shriek mark an' tried tae escyape;
It skipped ower the gyate tae the end of the field,
An' jigged oot the room wi' a spool an' a reel!
Follow the leader, Johnny me laddie,
Follow it through, me canny lad O;
Follow the transport, Johnny me laddie,
Away, lad, lie away, canny lad O!

(Industrial Ballad, Durham, N.E. England)

leading-edge *adj.*   **1** (Of a technology) a few microns blunter than STATE-OF-THE-ART. **2** (Of a tab-card feeding option) two of the eight possibilities. Whenever practical, tab cards should be submitted to the card reader so that the least significant columns are chewed up first.

lemma three *n.*   More strictly, a conjecture; even more strictly, a possible conjecture, insofar as Pierre de Fermat's dying words in 1665 were, "Ah, pauv'cons, you zink zat my penultimate conjecture was incroyable . . . *mais,* et c'est un grand *mais* . . . it is but un cas spécial of my jolie petite troisième lemmère, qu'on voit danser le long des golfes clairs . . . arrgh!" The search continues.

▶ CHORUS   Lèmma three, very pretty, and the converse pretty too;
But only God and Fermat knows which of them is true.

VERSE 1   When I studied number theory, I was happy in me prime,
And all them wild conjectures, I knocked them two at a time,
but . . .

CHORUS

VERSE 2   Last week at supervision, Max Newman said to me:
"Did you discover the deliberate mistake in lemma number three?"

CHORUS

VERSE 3   Lemma three it has puzzled mathematicians by the score,
But Max Newman has engulfed it, and it won't be seen no more.

CHORUS

VERSE 4   Well, the axiom of choice, it is very clear to me:
If you wanna choose a lemma, boys, then don't choose lemma three, for . . .

CHORUS

VERSE 5   And it's black and white together, we shall not be moved,
But the four-color theorem, it hasn't yet been proved, (last time . . .)

CHORUS   Lemma three, very pretty, and the converse pretty too;
But only God and Zeeman knows which of them is true.

less than *n.* *pronounced* $<$.\ A symbol of inequality having precedence over all other symbols of disparity.

▶The less than symbol is, typically, located between such pairs of variables as: {YOURDOXY, MYDOXY}, and {MYPAY, YOURPAY.}

lexicon *n.*   A small dictionary published by Irish Business Machines.

liberation *n.* [Latin *Liber* "a deity associated with the Greek Bacchus."] A specialized, heady form of emulation, allowing the user to switch rapidly from one manufacturer (usually IBM) to another (usually Honeywell) during an orgiastic half-price period known as the "happy hour."

LIFO *adj.* [Acronym for Last In, First Out.] **1** (Of a STACK) being analogous to the central deck of cards in gin rummy, where (pace card sharping) cards are taken from or placed on the top position only. As with gin rummy, the top item in the stack has usually been discarded by someone else and is not the item you are seeking. *Compare* FIFO; LINO in table of ACRONYMS. **2** (Of industrial relations) related to a commonly observed situation where the most recent employees are the first to strike.

linear programming *n.* *Also called* LP. A tidy method of programming in which the horizontal strings of source code are kept strictly parallel and right-hand justified, while all indentations are set to offer a pleasing trompe l'oeil vertical aspect.

◖Early, random tests by DPM proctors, aimed at eradicating insobriety and nonlinearity among programmers, included such odious practices as FORTRAN smear tests, SNOBOL uroscopies, and extended BASIC breathalyzers. The request to "blow into this bag" was often unsuccessfully countered by the rejoinder, "Why? Are your chips too hot?" The IUP (International Union of Programmers) has now negotiated a more humane regimen, whereby the proctor must have reasonable doubts regarding the state of the suspect programmer before demanding two simple, physical tasks: first, the programmer must circumnavigate a prescribed flowchart without vomiting; second, the programmer must thrice intone, without undue sibilation, "The LISP parenthesis doth perennially pisseth us off."

local *adj.* [Spanish *loco* "foolish, mad, irresponsible."] **1** (Of a site, terminal, node, branch, user, agent) being, rightly, kept in ignorance of the policies, strategies, and protocols devised, and daily refined, by some centralized pool of superior intelligence. **2** (Of a variable) confined; stunted; unable to spread its erroneous wings, and doomed to flap forever in some obscure, somber block. **3** (Of an error) latent; malignant; lurkful; ticking away. *Compare* GLOBAL.

logical diagram *n.* The graphical idealization of a circuit, indicating by means of lines, arrows, and symbols the various conflicting choices facing any electron rash enough to venture therein.

logomachy *n.* The good-humored altercation between supporters of EV-LISP and of EVQ-LISP.

♦As John McCarthy once said, "It doesn't really matter which language you choose; they're both very good."

loop *n. & v.intrans.* [From Middle English *loupe* "a noose, a circle of rope used in applied knot theory to enforce suspended judgments; a device similar to the one recommended by Polonius for garroting one's friends."] **1** *n. Programming* The frantic rehearsal of a certain sequence of program steps until the system "gets it right," failing which the loop is branded *endless;* the repetition of a certain sequence of program steps WHILE, and only while, a set of unforeseen circumstances prevails; an algorithmic recycling; a piece of code in search of a LOOPHOLE. **2** *n. Control theory* Also called **feedback loop.** The amplification and regurgitation of error signals in order to achieve any desired degree of instability. **3** *v.intrans. Programming* To relinquish command for an unspecified period, as: "D'you mind taking over the console, I'm looping for a while." *See also* DYNAMIC HALT; ENDLESS LOOP.

loop, endless *n.* *See* ENDLESS LOOP.

loophole *n.* **1** The escape route sought by a LOOP. **2** *Metacomputer science* The conceptual gap left when a loop migrates to another part of the metasystem. Any fresh loop nearby will be attracted into the hole, and so on. **3** *Marketing* A deficiency in the jurisprudential environment which allows overselling on the grounds of diminished responsibility, knowledge, and honesty.

Lord High Fixer *n.* For any given installation, the oldest living member of the original programming team.

♦Unfortunately, the Lord High Fixer, when needed, will be found to have moved to a distant, competitive site or to have set up as an independent consultant.

low-level language *n.* **1** A NATURAL LANGUAGE stripped of all semantic, morphological, and syntactical structure. **2** A primitive programming language in which each line of code needs, but never gets, 20 lines of comment. **3** *also called* **common language.** Imprecatory, often scatological strings aimed at an ailing system.

♦If delivered with sufficiently high DENIER, genuinely anthropomorphic venom, and heavy, reed-bending keyboard ostinato, such inputs have been known to shame the operating system into a belated response. The system's own obscure introspections will be suspended briefly while a conciliatory message is flashed to the user. *Compare* HIGH-LEVEL LANGUAGE.

LP *n.* [Long Playing.] Sometimes confused, understandably, with abbreviation for LINEAR PROGRAMMING.

Luddite *n.* [Origin: from "King" Ned Ludd, legendary victim of enforced automation during the Industrial Revolution, Yorkshire, England (ca. 1780).] One who, Canute-like, attempts to stem the tide of computerization. Having failed by stapling checks, folding tabcards, defacing OCR documents, demagnetizing credit cards, and part-paying utility and telephone accounts, the diehard Luddite resolves to continue the struggle from within by becoming an undercover programmer.

▶Ironically, most Luddite programmers quickly achieve DPM status, which denies them both the inclination and the opportunity to sabotage.

The Luddite class can kiss their ass,
I've got the foreman's job at last.

The DP counter-counterrevolution, though, must not become complacent. Three-shift vigilance should be the battle cry. Spotting the traitor coder in your midst is not easy—only the most naive Luddite will punch the giveaway X in column 5—since, nowadays, *all* programmers have the shifty, rebellious aspect of a communard freshly scraped off a disputed barricade, or the truculent sneer of one who has marched ten thousand miles to get to work. Similarly, the abnormality of program error distribution precludes any positive discrimination between *deliberate* and *standard* coding blunders.

Some overzealous vigilante groups still string up a suspect programmer at the drop of a label, and although several studies show this to be a cost-effective method of improving program quality (e.g., *Bonus Payments or Lynching?: A Comparative Study*—Judge Thumphreys, *Journal of the Institute for Software Productivity and Discipline,* vol. IX, no. 3, 1979), too many bright Luddites evade justice. Emerging as the least fallible indicator of the non-wasp in your system's bosom is the "punctuality test." Programmers consistently arriving on-site at the preordained time are doubly suspect. Why are they so anxious to "get at" the system? And how did they avoid the general state of abulia and debility induced in all genuine programmers by the previous session? Is there a time bomb ticking away in your cherished database? Your punctual, hard-working, overreliable apostates, they know, they know! Do not hang or fire them! Promote them quickly, the higher the better!

machine-independent *adj.* Being or pertaining to a software or hardware element which will not work on any computer.

MAFIA *n.* [Acronym for Mechanized Applications in Forced Insurance Accounting.] An extensive network with many on-line and offshore subsystems running under OS, DOS, and IOS.

▶MAFIA documentation is rather scanty, and the MAFIA sales office exhibits that testy reluctance to respond to bona fide inquiries which is the hallmark of so many DP organizations. From the little that has seeped out, it would appear that MAFIA operates under a nonstandard protocol, **OMERTA**, a tight-lipped variant of sna, in which extended handshakes also perform complex security functions. The known timesharing aspects of MAFIA point to a more than usually autocratic operating system. Screen prompts carry an imperative, nonrefusable weighting (most menus offer simple YES/YES options, defaulting to YES) that precludes indifference or delay. Uniquely, all editing under MAFIA is performed centrally, using a powerful rubout feature capable of erasing files, filors, filees, and entire nodal aggravations.

maintenance *n.* The replacement of one set of error states by another.

▶Ideally, the latter should be nonintersecting with, and more catastrophic than, the former. In *routine* maintenance this replacement is applied on a regular basis, so that DOWNTIME increases in an orderly, controlled, monotonic sequence. The system gracefully converges to a state of OBSOLESCENCE on a date convenient for the marketing department.

major new-level release *n.* 1 Any RELEASE. 2 The next release. 3 Level A128/12.456/K17C, replacing level A128/12.456/K17B. 4 A complete recasting of the systems software which renders all programs inoperative.

man-hour *n.* A sexist, obsolete measure of macho effort, equal to 60 kiplings.

◗One man-hour can represent one man working for an hour, two men quibbling for thirty minutes, or a billion men pussyfooting for a nanosecond. Most areas of DP activity now include a synergistic mix of male and female operatives, and the man-hour unit is being replaced by the PERSON-HOUR, using a conversion factor of 1.50.

MANIAC *n.* 1 An early computer built at the Institute of Advanced Studies, Princeton (fl. 1952). 2 "Anyone who has been making or using a digital computer for more than a few years."— *Faster than Thought,* Lord Bowden, 1953.

manufacturer *n. also (rare)* **supplier.** A loosely knit and constantly changing group referred to as "we" in proposals and "you" in legal actions.

◗More abstractly, the manufacturer is the second of the SEVEN CATASTROPHES OF COMPUTING. *See also* OEM.

map *n. & v.trans.* 1 *n.* The imponderable correspondence between two sets, one of which is unknown (called the *domain*), while the other (called the *range*) is unknowable. 2 *v.trans.* To establish, or to imagine the establishment of, some relationship between two incongruent sets, e.g., (disk sectors) to (bits), (sales territories) to (salespersons).

MBT *n.* [Memory Board Tagging.] (© Irish Business Machines). *See* PAGING.

mendacity sequence *n.* An ISO standard sorting sequence allowing the *F*'s in a truth table to be ordered by *degree* of falsehood.

◗The basic sequence, in ascending order, is: lies; damn lies; statistics; damn statistics; benchmarks; delivery promises; DP dictionary entries. Further refinements can be expected.

metaprogrammer *n.* Someone who is above programming but not yet ready for systems analysis.

◗ I met a programmer a-walking one day;
"O why aren't you coding?" to him I did say.
"I'm not a programmer, the truth I will tell,
But a metaprogrammer from meta-Ma Bell!"

CHORUS Sperry Rand, Rand, Rand, Sperry Rand.

VERSE 2   "Pray what do you do there?" the stranger I asked,
"And what are you paid for each tough meta-task?"
"I just *think* about programs," the young man did say,
"For a mere meta-pittance of twelve meta-K."

CHORUS

VERSE 3   "And where do you come from?" I finally cried.
"I come from Hell," the stranger replied.
"If you come from Hell, then tell me right plain
"How the hell you managed to get out again?"

CHORUS

VERSE 4   "The way I got out, Sir, the truth I will tell:
They're turning the systems folk all out of Hell;
This is to make room for the people who *sell,*
For there's a great number of them at Ma Bell."

CHORUS

VERSE 5   "Come all you salespersons, and take my advice;
Be fair to your prospects, and give a good price;
For if and you do not, I know very well,
You'll be in great danger of going to Hell!"

CHORUS

methodology *n.*   A method suffering from the prevalent 83 percent circumlocuflationary spiral.

MICR *n.* [Magnetic-Ink Character Recognition.] A system for bouncing checks of the wrong polarity.

micro- *adj.*   **1** Incredibly large with respect to the pico-. **2** Vanishingly small with respect to the giga-. **3** Quite normal in relation to objects of comparable scale.

microprocessor *n. & adj.*   **1** *n.* Twenty years of architectural bungling concentrated into a single chip. **2** *adj.* (Of a technology) relating to an approach which allows a single engineer to be replaced by a large-scale computer development team. *See also* EMULATION.

middle-out *adj.*   Relating to a new programming methodology allowing progress up or down as the mood of the team dictates. *Compare* BOTTOM-DOWN; BOTTOM-UP; TOP-DOWN.

◆The top-down/bottom-up schism is now confined to those computing backwaters where the DP VOGUE magazine arrives 2 weeks late. The middle-out approach allows an early, honest, and reassuring report to the DPM that the project is "definitely about halfway." The middle outer sees no contradiction in the proposition that one can break down vague tasks into precise subtasks and, at the same time, combine ill-conceived subroutines to form well-defined programs.

middleware *n.* 1 Les jarretelles noires de ma CORRECTRICE. 2 Les jarretelles rouges de ma correctrice. 3 Packages promulgated by independent middlepersons for the traditional 10 percent handling fee. 4 Les jarretelles blanches de ma correctrice.

◆At one time a well-defined partitioning of wariness could be discerned in the DP marketplace, but of late the question "who-does-what-with-what-to-whom-and-when" admits of no crisp resolution. *See also* OEM.

A sales pitch of daunting verbosity
Has dampened our mild curiosity;
Our spirits are quailed, for we were assailed
With wares of bewildering viscosity!

(M. Prospect Merrimé)

"Hardware, Software, Firmware, Middleware!
"The most important is to *be*-ware!"

(J. P. Sartrul)

mini-string *n.* [Origin: "When pain and anguish wring the brow,/ A mini-string Angel, Thou!"] *Also called* **G-string.** An expression of DENIER 14 or less, allowing a glimpse of the shape of strings to come.

MIPS *n.* [Acronym for Mega-Instructions Per Second.] An EPA-type assessment of CPU power, to be used for comparisons only. Your own performance will vary depending upon the bus driver, and will almost certainly be lower in California.

mnemonic *n.*

◆I had a wildly funny definition of this, but . . . oh, it may come back. . . .

modular *adj.* [Origin: Scottish proverb, "Mony a modular mickle maks a muckle."] 1 *Hardware* Heterogeneous; likely to disintegrate; pertaining to a device in which repairs are effected by changing every module. 2 *Software* Broken down; relating to a program which has been arbitrarily partitioned as a hedge against programming staff redundancies. *Compare* MONOLITHIC.

module *n.* [Latin *modulus* "a small measure."] **1** *Hardware* Any portion of a system that can fall off during shipment; any element in a system which can be replaced but not mended. **2** *Software* Any section of a program, known as a *discrete* module when supported by one programmer and as an *indiscreet* module when exposed to two or more programmers. *See also* MODULAR.

monolithic *adj.* Pertaining to a class of devices rendered obsolete by the invention of modularity. *Compare* MODULAR.

▶This demise is sad because when a monolithic unit broke down, the engineer simply changed the lith.

Monte Carlo method [Origin: after Count Montgomery de Carlo, Italian gambler and random-number generator (1792–1838).] A method of jazzing up the action in certain statistical and number-analytic environments by setting up a book and inviting bets on the outcome of a computation.

▶The count's original system was stolen by Lord Kelvin in 1901, and subsequently refined by Fermi, Ulam, and von Neumann during World War II to solve the many problems faced by belligerent neutrons in a game of Russian roulette. The Monte Carlo method spread like the vogue in the postwar United States, attracting, inevitably, an underground of seedy odds fixers, numbers racketeers, and heavy, protectionist muscle dons. The method is now banned outside Nevada, Atlantic City, and eponymous regions of Europe.

mount *v.trans.* [Origin: "Suffer the little peripherals to come unto Me"—St. Presper's *Sermon on the Mount.*] To expose (an item of hardware) to the vagaries of the software *or* to elicit the response that the specified item is unready or nonexistent.

MOZ DONG *n.* CURTATION of *Don Giovanni* by Wolfgang Amadeus Mozart and Lorenzo da Ponte, as performed by the computerized billing ensemble of the International Preview Society, Great Neck (sic), N.Y. See the illustration on the following page.

▶From Mozart to Edward Lear in one curtation, or as Fritz Spiegl once said, "From the sublime to the cor'blimey."

MSR *n.* Multiple-Source Responsibility. A major feature of the SNA protocol in the OEM environment. Under earlier SSR (Singular-

The International Preview Society
175 Community Drive, Great Neck, N.Y. 11025
PLEASE RETURN THIS PART OF INVOICE WITH YOUR PAYMENT

INVOICE FOR THIS SHIPMENT ONLY:

INVOICE DATE	CATALOG NUMBER	ALBUM TITLE	PRICE	POSTAGE AND HANDLING	SALES TAX	TOTAL PLEASE PAY THIS AMOUNT
02/09/78	476002	MOZ DONG +	8.98	1.09		10.07

Source Responsibility) implementations, the end user enjoyed but one, often receding, target for litigation. *See also* REVERSED CLASS ACTION.

MTBF *n.* [Mean Time Between Failure.]   A design parameter set by the manufacturer, based on the known tolerance of the user and the targeted profitability of the service department. *Compare* MTTR.

▶Manufacturers have long been aware that too high a value for the MTBF (measured, usually, in decades or fractions of decades) leads to a stultifying sense of boredom and complacency on the part of the user. The thoughtful supplier ensures that the user is exposed to the excitement of real breakdowns at reasonable intervals. Lifeboat-drill simulations are no substitute for that first actual mid-payroll catastrophe. The initial panic and wringing of throats soon gives way to the familiar elation of the front-line soldier under fire: sinews are stiffened, blood is summoned. On-site unity is magically rewoven as an almost forgotten camaraderie emerges to weather the blitz. "For the DPM shall lie down with the analyst, yea, even the programmer shall lie down with the punchperson." —St. Presper's *Epistolary Update to the Pascalites,* Level II, release ix. The traditional supplier/user frictions also, surprisingly, disappear, since the user is now, as it were, a born-again nonuser, and by definition a prospect for *something.* Long-forgotten salespersons will arrive to offer condolences and quotations for extended service: contracts, add-ons, standby units, upgrades, and newly released working software. Eventually, the peaceful boredom of uptime will be restored, prisoners exchanged, scapegoats tried and executed, memorials erected to lost files, and a candle placed on the console to honor the Unknown Coder. Years later, unblooded recruits will hold their manhoods cheap for missing the Great Crash of '78.

MTTR *n.* [Mean Time To Repair. Origin: *mean* "poor or inferior in grade or quality" + *repair* "to take off": as, "Let's repair to the bar."]   The possible sum of the following series, for which there are no easy convergence tests:

MTTNF	Mean Time To Notice Fault
MTTRTF	Mean Time To React To Fault
MTTLFEPN	Mean Time To Locate Field Engineer's Phone Number
MTTCFE	Mean Time To Call Field Engineer
MTAFECB	Mean Time Awaiting Field Engineer's Call Back
MTTCSC	Mean Time To Check Service Contract
MTTCFES	Mean Time To Call Field Engineer's Superior
MTTLTFEDBS	Mean Time To Listen To FE's Disclaimer Blaming Software
MTTCA	Mean Time To Call Attorney
MTFFETA	Mean Time For Field Engineer To Arrive
MTTD	Mean Time To Diagnose
MTTLTFEDBS	Mean Time To Listen To FE's Disclaimer Blaming Software
MTOOSCM × M#	Mean Time Ordering/Obtaining Software/ Changing Modules multiplied by number of modules
MTTRB	Mean Time To ReBoot
MTTRRB	Mean Time To ReReBoot

Gosub MTTD

⏵Some of the above labels, innocently though they fall on Indo-European ears, have offended Basque and Samoyed users. The Clean Up Naughty Tags committee of IFIP is frantically planning discussions for 1986. Watch this headword in future editions.

multi- *prefix* 1 Performing n functions or having n putative states, where $n \geq 2$: as, MULTIPROCESSING (read $\geq$ as "not much greater than"). 2 Performing no individual aspect of: as, MULTITASKING.

multijobbing *n.* Elementary moonlighting in which people modestly endeavor to widen their DP experience, in their free time, by assuming additional duties in disparate environments without boasting of their enterprise to their mainstream employer. *Compare* MULTITASKING.

◆Typically, the DPM at a Univac 1100 site could usefully multijob by becoming a covert third-shift operator at a nearby IBM 370 installation, and vice versa!

multiplex *v.trans.* [From *multi-* "slightly more than one" + contraction of *perplex* "to bewilder."]   To confuse (a device or person) by subdividing a problem and applying the pieces in parallel.

multiprocessing *n.*   The simultaneous processing of not many more than two portions of the same program on different units, e.g., on the mainframe CPU and the programmer's hand-held calculator.

multitasking *n.*   An advanced form of moonlighting in which the supplementary jobs are generated in a natural way from the multitasker's mainstream duties. *Compare* MULTIJOBBING.

◆Typically, a multitasking programmer will write packages during the day for his primary employer and spend the evenings correcting them at user sites as a freelance consultant.

MUM *n.* [Acronym for Multi-Use Mnemonics.]   A meta-mnemonic methodology whereby *one* acronym references *all* the features of a particular system.

◆Offsetting the advantage of having only one acronymic form to remember, there is, one is bound to admit, an attendant increase in ambiguity. In the case of the ETHELRED OS, for example, which vicariously assigns TPD to all aspects of the system, the MUM preamble points out that "the meaning of TPD is almost always clear from the context. The user should always use TPD (or the wild card *** which defaults to TPD) and trust the OS to apply the best guess." Current ISO regulations forbid the use of the acronym MUM *within* a MUM schema, although some churches allow a λ-MUM calculus whereby acronyms are distinguished from the names of the acronyms.

Murphy's law of programming [Formulated by H. Ledgard, 1975.]   "The sooner you start coding your program, the longer it is going to take."

MUSE *n.* [Acronym for Most Unusual Shakespearian Engine.]

> O! for a Muse of fire, that would ascend
> The brightest heaven of invent-i-on.
>
> —*Henry V*, W. Shakespeare

▶The author has proved elsewhere (*Computer Weekly,* March 6, 1969), with Rowsian certainty, that Shakespeare spent his 10 "missing" years, 1582–1591, developing MUSE, the first data processing system.

my program *n.* A gem of algoristic precision, offering the most sublime balance between compact, efficient coding on the one hand, and fully commented legibility for posterity on the other. *Compare* YOUR PROGRAM.

nack *n.* [Origin: corruption of vulg. *knackered* "castrated, rendered knackerless, impotentated."] A signal indicating that all is lost. *Compare* ACK.

nand *v.trans. & adj.* [Acronym for Not AND.] **1** *v.trans.* To unconjunct (several binary victims) in the boolean environment. **2** *adj.* (Of a GATE) being able to nand.

natural language *n.* **1** LISP (*see* table at ACRONYM) without the parentheses. **2** An overly high-level language lacking algorithmic precision and similar artificial additives, and therefore beyond the clutches of most compilers. *See* ENGLISH.

natural-language compiler *n.* The software required to *display* arbitrary PROMPTS on a terminal screen and *reject* the subsequent input strings (known as *responses*).

naturaller *adj.* (Of a computer language) gooder than natural; able to cope with the nuances of DP grammar.

nest *n. & v.trans.* [Origin: first used on English Electric KDF9 system, Kidsgrove, England (1962).] **1** *n.* A well-feathered STACK where data and instructions can be mother-henned and incubated for indefinite periods. **2** *v.trans.* To expose (loops, subroutines) to premature and/or unexpected CALLS. To each such exposure a positive integer, known as the *depth,* is assigned, indicating the approximate number of person-months needed to correct the situation.

> ♦ New string vests for ALGOL compilers;
> A night on the nest with the KDF9ers;
> Palimpsestuous programs with nebulous wings,
> These are a few of my favorite things.

netwok *n.* [Origin: a large Oriental colander.] A NETWORK running under the CHINESE VMOS protocol.

network *n. & v.trans.* [From *net* "reduced slightly from gross" + *work.*] **1** *n.* The antisynergetic interconnection of noncompatible nodal systems divided by a common protocol. **2** *v.trans.* To reduce [net] the work rate (of a computing resource) by adding it to a network.

NIH *adj.* [Abbreviation for Not Invented Here.] Pertaining to a much respected and widely practiced branch of design philosophy, unique among philosophical "schools" in that, by definition, the adherents refuse to talk to one another. Motivated by a fanatical hatred of plagiarism, NIH followers selflessly limit the domain of their responsibilities to their own humble artifacts. *See also* WHEEL.

Nobel Prize winners in computer science *n.* *See* NULL.

▶The nearest candidate for this honor was Sir Henry Ninebit-Byte (1912–1978), inventor of very wide paper tape, who was knighted in 1974 for "his invaluable services to the punch-card industry." His computerized Nobel Prize selection package was much admired until his own name occurred in five different categories during the 1977 dry run. Although he received the 1978 British Computer Society Silicon Medal for devious software, the Nobel scandal proved fatal, and he succumbed to a massive attack of disgrace.

noise *n.* **1** *Marketing* The raucous celebration of an order, aimed at swamping all signals from the design and manufacturing departments. **2** *Information theory* Illegible messages from Zatetic Venusians and Middle Earthers who have not yet mastered SNA.* **3** *Electronics* The thousand shades of grass that flesh is HAIR to.

non- *prefix.* A hint that the following attribute or device is not available for immediate delivery, but that a sufficiently firm letter of intent might well secure a less dogmatic evaluation leading to a favored position in the waiting list. *Compare* NOT-; UN-.

nor *v.trans. & adj.* [Acronym for Not OR.] **1** *v.trans.* To undisjunct (several binary victims) in the boolean environment. **2** *adj.* (Of a GATE) being able to nor.

not- *prefix.* The positive, unswerving negation of the ensuing concept. *Compare* NON-; UN-. *See also* HOLE.

---

*Likewise, some claim that cosmic rays are failed experiments in beaming down visitors from outer space.

♦Babbage's memory boards relied on timber crosscuts with granular singularities known as *knot-holes*. Subsequent confusion when this technique was transferred to slices of silicon led to the corruption *not-holes*.

null

♦

number cruncher *n.* A heavy device for testing the compressibility of numbers. The traditional method, pioneered by Control Data Corporation, is to subject each number to progressively denser FORTRAN programs until all 60 bits squeak.

numerolatry *n.* The unhealthy obsession with numbers and numerical precision; the use of computers in the social sciences. *See also* INCH WORM.

numerology *n.* The recreational branch of computer science.

♦Among the many deep DP theorems in the numerological environment, we cite:

1. The CDC 7600 is four times as powerful as the ICL 1900.

2. The computer in the film *2001* was an IBM degrade:

   (IBM − 111 = HAL)

3. The English Electric LEO3 was an upgrade of the KDN2:

   (KDN2 + 111 = LEO3)

4. Donald Knuth's renowned MIX was "the world's first polyunsaturated computer. Like most machines, it has an identifying number—the 1009. This number was found by taking 16 actual computers which are very similar to MIX and on which MIX can be easily simulated, and then averaging their numbers with equal weight:

   $$\lfloor (360 + 650 + 709 + 7070 + U3 + SS80 + 1107 + 1604 + G20 + B220 + S2000 + 920 + 601 + H800 + PDP4 + II)/16 \rfloor = 1009$$

   The same number may also be obtained in a simpler way by taking Roman numerals."—Donald E. Knuth, *The Art of Computer Programming, Fundamental Algorithms,* vol. 1, Addison-Wesley Publishing Company, Inc., Reading, Mass., 1968.

5. The Sperry Univac series 90 furnishes IBM series 360 performance with a 75 percent cost reduction.

object *n.* *Also called* **object code.** [Latin *obicio, obiectum* "reproach, be-grudge."] The compacted, illegible version of the SOURCE CODE grudgingly produced by an assembler or compiler.

▶Object code is sometimes correctly referred to as "binary," but it is considered impolite to call it "machine code" or "machine language" without first checking with the machine.

obsolescence *n.* A system state determined exclusively by the manufacturer's marketing department.

▶Users are strongly advised not to attempt this diagnosis unaided. Obsolescence depends on many factors known only to the sales force—the cost prices and margins on each model, whether all the available options have been added on to meet the original performance targets, the degree to which the user is locked in, and so on. In fact, the user can be assured that the supplier *and* the supplier's competitors will be quick to spot the first symptoms and will lose no time in bringing the matter to the DPM's attention. The news of impending obsolescence induces a menopausal shock in some users, but there is really no rational basis for panic. Studies have shown that the onset of obsolescence invariably coincides with the launching of a new and better system. The angst of the user is soon swept away by the excitement of conversion and the challenge of incompatibility.

OCR *n.* [Optical Character Recognition.] A method for misreading source documents directly into a system without having to mispunch cards first.

OCR A *n.* [So named because every character looks like an A.] A typeface designed to be illegible to humans but unreadable by OCR scanners.

OCR B *n.* An improvement on OCR A whereby human legibility is improved at the expense of OCR scanner performance. *Compare* E13B.

oedipos complex *n.* [Blend of *Oedipus* + *OS* "operating system."] The fears developed during the first 3 to 6 years' exposure to a domineering operating system, especially by the male user, that his algorithmic potency is threatened by arbitrary job truncation. *See also* OSOPHOBIA.

OEM *n.* [Obscure Equipment Methodology, or *rare* Original Equipment Manufacturer.]

▶The computer manufacturer has, from the genesis of the trade in the 1950s, faced three major hazards: making computers, selling them, and effecting installation. The OEM approach, evolved gradually during the natural struggle to reduce costs and responsibilities, has virtually eliminated all three problems. Manufacturers no longer make computers, but rather assemble each other's MODULES. The modules are in their turn produced by obscure specialist companies from submodules provided by obscurer suppliers, and so on ad nauseam, through an infinitely parasitic hierarchy. Likewise, the selling and installing chores have been increasingly delegated to systems houses, software houses, and houses of mixed repute; consultants, both freelance and respectable; and a variety of mail-order medicine persons, itinerant street vendors, and friendly neighborhood haberdashers. Knitting this fine fly-by-night web together, and tempting the user into the many-mansioned parlor of automation, is SNA (Scapegoat Network Architecture). In the likely event of trouble, the end user simply removes the five superimposed decals from each offending component, providing at least 20 defendants for a dramatic REVERSED CLASS ACTION.

OEM cogs *n.* The main reason why Charles Babbage's Analytical Engine (c. 1834) failed to perform to specification, and why his "mill did grind exceeding slow."

office use only *n.* A blank area left on TURNAROUND documents for subsequent OCR encoding should the LUDDITES fail to strike first.

▶There are two schools of thought on how best to discourage the great unwashed public from defacing turnaround documents. The total failure of simple "Do not use this space" warnings has persuaded some form designers to omit all such legends, while others have elected to provide a variety of "decoy" boxes with caveats calculated to invite graffiti from the most staid recipient, but craftily protecting the real sacrosanct areas. The growing complexity of actual and pseudo admonishments is illustrated by the following example:

O C R area !!!!!

We URGE you, PLEASE, not to DEFACE this space in any way!!!

H O N E S T L Y this **REALLY** is I M P O R T A N T .

IF you feel you must record telephone numbers, shopping lists, or simply doodle in this virgin area, PLEASE use only a soft pencil (2B or less) avoiding all the characters listed overleaf. Whatever you do, for GOD's sake avoid the symbol ■ OR ANYTHING REMOTELY LIKE IT. You've no idea the chaos this one causes. Look, we know you hate computers. D'you think *we* like them? We're just as much locked into the system as you are. So, give us a break, man. THANKS FOR YOUR COOPERATION.

Ogam *n.* *also called* **Ogham**.   An early (800 B.C.) Celtic version of the ASCII character set, designed for epigraphic efficiency but often observed on CRT displays. See the illustration on page 95.

one-line patch *n.* [From D. C. Moulton, Ilford, Essex, England.] A KLUDGE so minimal that no testing is necessary. Corrected by a further one-line patch. *See* RECURSION.

open *adj. & v.trans.* **1** *adj.* (Of a file) exposed, at risk. **2** *adj.* (Of a loop) endowed with a loophole. **3** *v.trans.* To render (a file) vulnerable to subsequent reads, writes, and kills; to invoke the message "file does not exist" or "file already open." **4** *v.trans.* To depress (a meeting) with a few well-chosen introductory remarks while coffee cups and fees are being collected. **5** *v.trans.* To steal the password (of an account); to make (a sesame) open.

operating system *n.*   That part of the system that inhibits operation. *Also called* OS (from the clothing industry's abbreviation for *outsize*).

▶In metacomputer science, great care is needed to distinguish: (1) the OS qua OS, (2) the name of the OS, viz., < OS > , (3) what we call the name

	Europe		North America				Ogam Tract No. 3	
Letter	Ireland Ogam Tract No. 16	Portugal, Cachão da Rapa	Vermont	Connecticut, Massachusetts, New Hampshire	Inwood, New York	Oklahoma, Texas, Arkansas, the Caribbean	Ireland	Monhegan, Maine
		[Pontotoc, Oklahoma, also]						
H								
D								
T								
C			Uses G					
Q								
B								
L								
F/V								
S								
Ñ			Uses N̄					
M								
G								
Ñ								
Z			Lacking					
R			Uses L					
Ia, Ea								
W, Ui			?			[or]		

Early Ogam alphabets of Europe and North America. The oldest styles employ only consonants, and appear to date from around 800 B.C. onward. The fully developed Irish style, with vowels and the whole range of consonants, appears only in monuments believed to postdate the time of Christ.

of the OS, viz., " <OS> ," (4) what the OS calls itself, viz., { " <OS> " }, and (5) what the OS calls when it calls itself, viz., " < { " <OS> " } > "

operator *n.* [Origin doubtful: possibly Italian *opera* "a long, boring concatenation of overdramatic, far-fetched, hysterical, and contradictory incidents," or, less plausible: Latin *opus* "work."]   The lowest and least dispensible (*archaic* "dispensable") link in the system's pecking order. *See* PRECEDENCE.

▶Spotters' Club hint: Look out for the ill-clad person reading the sports pages and flicking cigarette ash in the card-reader hopper.

OR *n.* [Origin: possibly English *or* "offering a choice," or abbreviation for **O**perations **R**esearch (Brit: **O**perational **R**esearch).]

1 An alternative to planning. **2** An indiscipline aimed at attracting mathematicians from Academia so that they can mop up all surplus computing resources in the commercial sector.

▶Among the top 50 fortune-seeking corporations, the OR department has replaced the DAT box as the most cherished status symbol.

or *v.trans. & adj.* [Origin: English conj. *or* ≈ "alternative."] **1** *v.trans.* To disjunct (several binary victims) in the boolean environment. **2** *adj.* (Of a GATE) being able to or. *Compare* AND; NAND; NOR.

OS *n.?* or *adj.?* *pronounced* oz\\ Possible abbreviation for **OutSize** or **Operating System**, *or* from French *os* "bone," as, "J'ai un os à gratter avec vous." *See* OPERATING SYSTEM.

osophobia *n. DP psychiatry* The morbid fear of OPERATING SYSTEMS.

▶A doctor writes: "Except in extreme cases, this condition should not give rise to undue concern or bills exceeding $5000. There can be few normal persons who have not, at one time or another, recoiled in horror when confronted with a 20K supervisor. I know I have. DP Freudians have created their usual catchdollar theories to exploit the gullible osophobic. They equate the monitor with some tyrannical father figure bent on castrating both program and programmer, and bestow grotesque phallic tokens on such innocent, mundane concepts as "input," "output," "random access," "nesting," "multiple job streams," and "first-in-last-out." The ultimate folly in this verbose quackery was a recent paper presented at a Jungian Institute seminar on "Spooling Dysfunctions and the OEDIPOS COMPLEX," which attempted to correlate instances of golf-ball printer failures with a symbolic (sic) increase in the male operators' anxiety state. As I indicated earlier, there are, alas, extreme sufferers beyond the pale and budget of medical science. We take them away from SCOPE and GEORGE III as soon as we can, although little remains for them but a few twilight years in the Thumps Memorial Home for the Recursively Bemused." *See also* ETHELRED OS.

overflow *n. & v.* **1** *n.* A binary spillage. "Overflow is never having to say, 'endloop.' " **2** *v.trans.* To exceed the capacity (of a register, file, listener) in order to test the overflow indicator. **3** *v.trans.* To produce more FLOWCHARTS than the site walls can support.

▶ . . . Enough! no more:
Your bits are dripping on the floor.

> —*Twelfth Shift; or, What Next*

See BIT BUCKET.

overheads *n.pl.* **1** *Conversation* Metaremarks, richly laced with metajargon, helpfully aimed at deflating, eviscerating, decapitating, and pronouncing dead any listeners reluctant to admit their obvious intellectual and experiential inferiority. "This may be a little over your heads, but. . . ." **2** Excesses in the oralistic environment. **3** The expenses incurred in producing the eponymous visual aids. **4** *DP accounting* For a given installed and running system: the total cost of manufacturing, labor, components, delivery, software support, service during the guarantee period, documentation, initial supplies (including the unbilled ribbon accidentally delivered with the line printer), sales commissions and expenses, and bribes.

oxymoron *n.* The concatenation of *m* strings in an *n*-valued logic $(1 < m \leq n)$ where no two strings have the same truth-value.

▶In the 2-valued logic endured by most readers (*see* BINARY), the oxymoron is daily fact of life:

TABLE OF OXYMORONS

operating system

PROG. RUN

delivery date

job satisfaction

final version

supporting documentation

comprehensive package

management function

long-term benefit

backup copy

systems analysis

structured environment

benchmark results

salesforce responsibility

package switching *n.* **1** The conversion, following threats of litigation, from one set of stolen programs to another. **2** A cryptogrammic technique which, rather than recoding characters in a message, achieves mystification by directing arbitrary partitions of the message to random locations. *See also* EPSS.

paging *n.* **1** *Communications* A panic call for the person who has just left the site and is rushing to reach the nearest bar beyond the radius of the paging system. **2** *Software* A VIRTUAL memory management system pioneered on the Ferranti Atlas computer (1958) and rediscovered by IBM in 1976 in which the system flicks or browses through numbered sections of mass storage (known as pages) until one catches its fancy. As with Mr. Caxton's invention, there is a high probability of accessing a few well-worn pages (known as the "dirty bits").

▶Irish Business Machines pioneered a hardware page location method (1980) called MBT (Memory Board Tagging) whereby the corners of the memory boards are bent over to speed a second access.

Le livre s'ouvre seul au feuillet souvent lu.

E. Rostand, *L'Aiglon*

paper low *n.* A lamp which lights to indicate that your output is now appearing on the PLATEN.

parallel *n. & adj.* **1** *n.* An unheeded warning; a disaster occurring elsewhere but discounted by an unwise appeal to Euclid's fifth postulate; the woes of others which remain at a constant distance, however prolonged. **2** *adj.* Being or pertaining to everything happening at once. "When sorrows come, they come not single spies, but in battalions."—*Hamlet. Compare* SERIAL.

parentheses *n.pl.* (A (pair (of symbols (referred to as (open) and (closed))) each) of which) has the (hold (down) ((to)(repeat) option) on a ((LISP)-(oriented) keyboard)). *See* table of ACRONYMS.

parenthesis *n.* *Archaic* singular of PARENTHESES.

◗In most respectable languages, a singular, unmatched bracket is syntactically inadmissible.

parity *n. & adj.* [From *parrot* "to repeat without understanding."] **1** *n.* A state of bankruptcy achieved by installing the same computer system used by your nearest competitor. **2** *adj.* (Of a check) able to detect an odd number of bit mutilations but oblivious to the equally probable situation in which an even number of bits get splayed.

Pascal manual *n.* Any book with an introduction by Prof. N. Wirth.

password *n.* **1** The user's first name, or the first four characters of the user's first name. **2** A widely known sesame that suddenly becomes widely forgotten. **3** The string contained in the single-element file called "**X**" where X is the string held in the single-element file called **PASWRD**. **4** A device aimed at encouraging free and open cooperation among the staff.

patch *n. & v.trans.* [From JARGON FILE.] **1** *n.* A temporary addition to a piece of code, usually as a quick and dirty remedy for an existing bug or misfeature. A patch may or may not work, and may or may not be eventually incorporated permanently into the program. **2** *v.trans.* To insert a patch (into a piece of code).

pause *n.* **1** A pleasant period of inactivity with unfortunate side effects called DELAY. **2** A regular 5-second interval during which networks suspend operations to "allow local stations to identify themselves," after which regular programming is resumed.

payroll *n.* [From *pay* "emolument" + *roll* "to stagger, to perform a periodic revolution."] **1** A computer run that allows you to see how much more your colleagues are making and, in extreme cases, offers remedial action via discreet program optimization. **2** The most vulnerable business application, and therefore the first to be computerized.

◗The vulnerability of an application is measured by the adverse impact of its output on the recipients. Programs which output only to their case-hardened programmers can be considered nonvulnerable. Those applications producing reports for top and middle management can be rated 10 to 20 percent vulnerable, since such listings are mainly cosmetic in character, and if they should accidentally trigger management decisions, the vulnerability factor can quickly be lowered by more severe curtation of the report heading legends and an oppressive increase in report output volume. Together, these improvements restore the normal, harmless interdepartmental listings shuffle by bemused managers, bring welcome overtime for the shredding-machine minders, and provide a happy boost to the paper-salvage account.

Billing systems, on the other hand, carry a 50 to 70 percent vulnerability rating. Suspicious, testy outsiders, known as customers, receive computerized invoices showing wrong extensions for unordered items, mismatching statements, and prematurely threatening letters.

Fortunately, most customers are equally computerized, and this reduces the human involvement as the vendor's accounts receivable package clashes head on with the vendee's accounts payable package.

The vulnerability of the billing system is also reduced by the physical separation of the contenders, but no such lack of contiguity protects the poor payroll. The scurvy, plebeian payee sweats and grunts *within sight* of the strutting, cossetted DP overlords and their expensive artifacts. Payroll errors are no mere academic debating points. The workers know their gross and net dues to the finest floating point, and are seldom placated by some bearded discourse on the misplaced GOSUB in line 4567 of the FICA SICK DED routine. Also, perhaps to a greater extent than any other computer application, including intercontinental missile guidance, the payroll is ultra time-critical. The minutest aberration in meeting the inexorable payroll deadline enrages the grasping employees. They will, at the drop of a W2, storm the computer room, armed with distraught relatives and pellagrous children, creating a far from ideal environment for the programmer who is trying to understand and incorporate the latest batch of changes from the IRS. A revival of one of the many successful ancient systems of slavery seems the only solution.

peer group *n.* [From *peer* "observe closely" + (mathematics) *group* "a set closed under a given operation."] All those stupid enough to claim equal status and rash enough to pass judgment.

personal computing *n.* A literally in-house database management system managed by the head of the household, who, singly, assumes the duties of procurement committee, purchasing officer, DPM, systems analyst, programmer, data preparation department, field service engineer, goods inward, and accounts payable. The roles of end user, Luddite, and Job's comforter are played, vari-

ously, by the kids, spouse, and neighbors. Often contrasted with
IMPERSONAL COMPUTING, where the owners have no direct involvement or enthusiasm.

◗The growing success of personal computing is due to the users' lack of
formal DP expertise, the reduced need to delegate, and the freedom from
artificially frenetic deadlines. Personal computing has replaced personal
transportation, not only in the number of magazines on the newsstands,
but as the topic of party small talk:

"What are you driving now?"

"Oh, I drive a pair of Helios-2 disks with a voice-coil device. Only
750K, but terrific access time. I traded my cassettes in only last month
. . . ."

"Really? I've just splashed out on a CDC Hawk, 10.6 *marvellous* megs,
you know, and a lot more than I really need, but the wife absolutely
fell for that cartridge blue . . . ."

". . . and how *is* Melinda? Haven't seen her since that *divine* Palo Alto
core swap . . ."

". . . she's fine, but stubborn as ever. I can't get the dumb bitch to
switch from *Basic,* would you believe? We had a simply disastrous
evening last week; a combined Tupper and software party . . . she sold
five dinner sets and three floppy disk holders . . . but my Snobol
biorhythm dem went completely wild . . . so embarrassing. . . ."

". . . those DP turkeys at the office, struggling along with a 360/20;
they used to pull the wool over my eyes . . . now they're all lining up
outside my garage with their silly little Fortran jobs. . . . "

person-hour *n.* A unit of work effort replacing the obsolete MAN-
HOUR. A conversion factor of 1.50 should be applied. *Also called*
labor-hour.

pessimizing compiler [From JARGON FILE.] A compiler that pro-
duces object code that is worse than the straightforward or obvious translation.

phase *n. & v.trans.* [From JARGON FILE.] 1 (Of people) the phase of
one's waking-sleeping schedule with respect to the standard 24-
hour cycle.

◗A person who is roughly 12 hours out of phase is said to be "in night
mode." Changing one's phase can be effected in two ways; the "hard
way" is to stay awake for a long period, while the "easy way" is to stay
asleep until the appropriate SHIFT is attained.

2 (Of the moon) *also called* POM. A random parameter upon which something is said, humorously, to depend, implying either the unreliability of whatever is dependent, or that its reliability seems to be dependent on conditions still to be determined, as: "This feature depends on having the channel open in mumble mode, having the foo switch set, and on the phase of the moon." 3 *v.trans.* To declare, without warning, (a product or feature) to be mandatory (phase in) or obsolete (phase out).

pigeonhole *n. & v.trans.* [Origin: painful contraction of *pigeon's hole.*] 1 *n.* An appropriate destination for most data, cheaper than sorting and limited in capacity only by the size and courage of the pigeon. 2 *v.trans.* To cram (data, documents, opinions) into a pigeonhole.

◗This sadistic data-partitioning methodology was developed in England in the 1850s, jointly by the Common Carrier Pigeon Breeders' Association and the RSPB (the Royal Society for the Prevention of Birds), at the request of the military, who were seeking an improved communications technology to help resolve the Crimean stalemate. The need to transmit dispatches too boring to fit the leg jacket of the average *Columbus tabellarius simplexicus,* and the increasing point-to-point distances to be covered as the anti-Russian alliance eased its way to Sevastopol, invoked the breeding of several large-ringed hybrids, the *C. superanalidae,* for example, and the delicate refinement of in-flight package switching. The instructive experimental errors of that period still survive in current DP jargon. One particularly decimating link in the ARPA network is reverentially known as the "valley of death," and users often say they "get a charge" from certain protocolic idiosyncrasies which lead to fatal transmission errors.

platen *n.* A supplementary print spooling device which can retain, typically, 20 lines of print in the absence of paper.

◗An engineer writes: "The effectiveness of your platen as an emergency print buffer is much improved by regularly cleaning it with a soft, damp rag. The proper frequency will depend on the alertness of your paper-feeding staff and the sensitivity of the paper-low warning system. Note that printing on the platen is cumulative, rather than clear-before-write. If more than, say, three buffer cycles occur before the nonpaper situation is detected, the chances of recovery are rather slight. A notable exception was the painstaking study of ST. PRESPER's ancient IBM typewriter—the famous decipherment of the Dead-C platen—which miraculously recovered most of that absent-minded anchorite's unpublished scriptures.

The suggestion that platens and printer ribbons should be of contrasting colors is being actively debated by 28 of the affected standards committees.

plotter *n.*   The device or person after your job.

poaching *n.*   *Marketing* The stochastic enlargement of a prospect set in order to solve certain formulations of the TRAVELING SALESPERSON PROBLEM.

♦In lenient 19th-century England, poachers were given a free cruise to Van Diemen's Land; in the harsher commercial climate of today, poachers find themselves transported to hellish weekend Quota-makers' Conventions in Cleveland.

Polish notation *n.*   [Latin *politus* "refined, elegant."]   A notation for those unable to pronounce Lukasiewicz, but anxious to pay homage to his native land.

♦Sometimes *(vulg.)* spoken of as Okie notation, English notation, Papist notation, and so on, depending upon the local subculture and/or the courage of the speaker.

POM *n.*   [From JARGON FILE.]   Acronym for PHASE OF THE MOON. *Chiefly,* as: "POM dependent," flaky, unreliable.

PPN *n.*   *pronounced* pippin or pay-pay-en\\   Abbreviation for Project Programmer Number (DEC, Alphamicro, etc.) or French "Il ne Passera Pas la Nuit" (i.e., close to death).

prayer *n.*   A low-cost method of data verification, the efficiency of which depends on the intensity, sincerity, and accuracy of the supplicant, and on the mood of the Beseeched.

♦A DP theologian writes: "In the early 1950s, input to the EDSAC I at Cambridge University, England, was punched on blind (no hard copy) five-channel CREED paper-tape perforators. Try telling that to this year's graduates . . . they just won't believe you. The LAW OF VOLTAIRE-CANDIDE was some consolation, insofar as 5 channels offered only 32 code combinations, which greatly reduced the chance of error. The old figs/letters trick increased the repertoire to 58 codes or so, still far below what the ASCII-pampered kids of today take for granted. In the absence of paper-tape verifiers, the prayer method of verification was devised and used even by the Marxian majority. It was widely argued that IF God existed, He or She would be a Cantabrigian, ELSE Lenin might be listening, ELSE only a few minutes in the long input cycle would be lost in any event. The choices of Deity and timing (for maximum receptivity) were subject to many informal benchmarks. Needham's successes seemed to favor the standard Church of England Trinity, Whose lines were busy only during a few peak Sunday festivals. Composite entreaties to mixed lists of pre-, pro-, and post-Christian gods were the least effective, supporting the thesis that the Omnipotent are overpoweringly jealous of one another. Those wishing to take up the prayer method of verification are strongly advised to pick one One, forsake the rest, truly believe, and shun apostasy. Two thoroughly tested specimen prayers follow. Substitute your preferred values for the God-string variables X, Y, and Z, and feel free to vary the degree of obsequiousness according to your personal tastes.

Prayer A:—(X should have a Christian-type value.) "O dearly beloved yet feared X, cast Thou Thine penetrating glance upon these our data, and grant them, O X, Thy powerful chastising and corrective methodologies, for there is no good in them; for we have punched the things we ought not to have punched; and we have skipped the things we ought to have punched. O X, before Whom all systems tremble, forgive, we beseech Thee, the manifold trivialities of our appointed tasks, but nonetheless guide them safely through our Vale of Tears Mk. I, that our output may glorify Thy Name. Finally, O X, if Thou hast a free moment, we beg Thee, before we submit this unworthy tape unto Thy stabilizing mercy, that Thou mightst quickly review our new level 3.4 operating system, many features of which find Thy children sorely tried, yea even untried. For what we sowed in haste, reap we now in endless patches. Fix Thou, we pray, our bountiful oversights, that we might lift up our overall performance, whence cometh our income. And all this we ask in Thy name, as ordained in Thy many exciting newsletters. Amen."

Prayer B—(Set X to any suitable male Greek value in the Olympian environment, and let Y = a mother of a wife of X.) "Brave, wise, openeyed X; yes, you who rescued Zilicon unchipped from the dull-brown earth, snatched Taenia and Papyros from the river's edge. Kind regards to your wives and families! It's some time since we enlisted your help. Too long, unaided, have we engaged in perilous, uncharted programs, stormtossed voyages on standby, plagued with Tyche's bugs, while encoding the extant sagas of your forgotten followers and translating them into contemporary English. Are we reaching you, allhearing X? Show us a sign! A thunderbolt to smite our unreliable oracle would not displease some sections of this camp. Nor would we object to the immediate destruction of the enemy's seer, who struts within the shadow of our spears. The ships charged with our night-watch relief languish windless on a distant bay. Three and thrice three shifts have sleepless passed since first we went on-line. Our IO, once so fair, is a complete cow, and we suspect that the branchtongued Y

is compounding our woes! Clearsighted X, guide this reel of entrail, freshly plucked, which we reluctantly fling at our sleeping oracle."

precedence *n.* **1** *DP sociology* The natural, calvinistically ordained pecking order, as

Systems analysts and your ladies,
Consultants and your mistresses,
PRs and your roommates,
Salesmen and your bits on the side,
Programmers and your wives,
Operators and your women,
Be upstanding and raise your glasses!
I give you IBM, free enterprise, and sexual equality!

—Anonymous Computer Society Toastmaster

2 *Mathematics* Arbitrary rules allowing the evaluation of

$$2 + 3 \times 6 / 4 \uparrow 9 - 1$$

and similar puzzles.

◗It's always a good idea to check out the rules prevailing in your particular system, and to use brackets in any case.

prefix notation *n.* Reversed SHILOP notation.

prestidigit *n.* [Latin *praestigiator* "conjurer, magician" + *digit.*] **1** A numerical character located in VIRTUAL memory. **2** An amazing disappearing trick performed with a push-down STACK.

price/performance *n.* A ratio which allows chalks and cheeses to be compared with any desired degree of arithmetical precision.

◗A test-nonzero on the denominator is recommended.

prime rate *n.* A monotonic, increasing sequence of interest percentages devised by bankers to discourage, gently but firmly, the greed of their clients. The rates follow the well-known series: 2, 3, 5, 7, 11, 13, 17, 19, . . . , and it is conjectured that, in the endless struggle to combat inflation, the prime-rate increment need not exceed 2 points on an infinite number of opportunities.

proctologist *n.* [From Greek *proktos* "rectum" + *logos* "word."] One who is involved in, or intrigued by, the output problem.

program *n. & v.* **1** *n.* A PROGRAMME written in a lower-level language, such as American English. **2** *n.* A sequence of detectable and undetectable errors aimed at coaxing some form of response from the system. **3** *v.trans.* To match (a problem) with the least inappropriate COMPUTIBLE function. *See also* COMPUTABLE. **4** *v.trans.* To write programs with no particular object in mind. *See* HEURISTICS.

◗Programs are graded according to the response elicited:

Program Grade	Response
A	Rejection with diagnostics
B	Rejection—no reason given
C	Total indifference

Recent rumors that ISO is mooting a grade A+ for programs which evoke parts of the desired output were greeted with good-natured derision by the programming community. A spokesperson for the IUP (International Union of Programmers) declared that "this unwarranted arousal of our employers' expectations will unconditionally increment the invidiousness of our members, already grappling with badly defined problems under adverse environments. Brothers and sisters, this new grading puts us all on the thin slope of a most slippery wedge!" The cheering delegates then spontaneously took up Chant #215 from the **IUP** Hymnal:

Hey, hey, Thomas J.,
How many files did ya lose today?
Bricks without straw, that's OK;
Bricks without clay,
No way!!!

programania *n.* An incurable type of megalomania in which the sufferer, possessed of demoniac stamina and oblivious to budgetary constraints, attempts to prove that all problems can be solved by computer.

◗A DP doctor writes: "The Thumps Memorial Home for the Recursively Bemused (Stockport, England) reports that 90 percent of its cubicles are now occupied by irremediable programaniacs. The Home's 370/168 is well beyond the normal three-shift saturation point, but the inmates appear to be willing to accept almost any TSO indignity in their futile search for the universal algorithm. 'They are all model patients,' quipped Home Director Dr. Hermes, 'and God knows you need patience with the model we bought.'

My own practice handles mainly academic sufferers on an outpatient basis. These sad cases have exhausted their campus budgets, and many drift into a life of crime: forging account numbers, stealing passwords, panhandling the computer allocation committee—"Can you spare a time slice and a couple of K? Look, man, I ain't had a decent run all week"— raiding Byte Shops, freaking Telenet, and so on. There isn't a lot I can do. I have a few Apples in the clinic, but not much core. If I try to wean them off DP with some old-fashioned basket weaving, they immediately want to automate the basket weaving with some grandiose occupational therapy package. Since I started putting my appointments and billing on my computer, I find I can spare less and less time with my patients. . . ."

programme *n.* A PROGRAM written in English.

programmer *n.* 1 One who claims or appears to be engaged in the perpetration of programs. 2 The systems analyst's diplomatic attaché at the alien court of the CPU. 3 One engaged in a practical, nonsystematic study of the halting problem. 4 "A harmless drudge."—Lord Bowden, 1953.

prompt *n.* A delayed message from the system demanding an immediate response from the user.

proposal *n.* 1 *Staff relations* A suggestion aimed at reducing third-shift ennui. 2 *Marketing* A standard set of binders submitted by the manufacturer to the prospect in which the first page of volume I is personalized with the prospect's name and the last page of volume III is personalized with a quotation.

proposal evaluation *n.* 1 *Staff relations* The slight pause between PROPOSAL and acceptance. 2 *Marketing* The weighing of manufacturers' proposals by the prospect.

◆Conventional postal scales will cope with all but the most outrageous proposals. The Horchow catalogue, however, does offer an up-market proposal evaluator in polished brass with logarithmic scale which will handle multivolume proposals in a single pass. After weighing each proposal, the next step is to compute the ratio (Total net $ quotation)/(weight of proposal in pounds). The four bidders with the lowest ratios are then informed that they are in the short list of three. Current ISO standards allow from one (minimum) to seven (maximum) proposers to be admitted to the "short list of three," but experience indicates that nominating four, if possible, ensures continued goodwill and dilutes any accusation of bias. Further pruning of the short list is best left to the infallible and ineffable forces of economics and nepotism.

proprietary caveat *n.* [From Latin *proprius* "one's own" + *caveat* "let him/her beware," whence = "let the owner beware."] *Software* The quasi-legalistic preamble appended to unbundled programs, which, like the Ten Commandments, serves as the sinner's vade mecum:

◖Software caveats, ideally, should be limited to 10 percent of the total source code, but the experienced user expects all worthwhile piratic opportunities to be included.

prospect *n.* [Latin *prospectā re* "to look forth upon."] **1** One of the real visitational targets in the TRAVELING SALESPERSON PROBLEM. **2** A company or individual temporarily unable to contact a reference account. **3** Anyone who circles a number on a magazine reader service card. *Compare* INTROSPECT; SUSPECT.

PTF *n.* [Permanent Temporary Fix, or *rarely* Program Temporary Fix.] Any programming action taken to bypass software errors reported by a field engineer.

◖Program Temporary Fix was an early IBM euphemism for a PATCH. Any PTF which offers immediate mollification of the bug or misfeature stands a good chance of being incorporated into the definitive system's corpus. Subsequent side effects can be blamed on the original error.

punch *n. & v.trans.* **1** *n.* A device used to reduce the weight of a card or paper tape in order to minimize postal charges. The CHADIC by-products have proved to be a useful and persistent confetti. **2** *v.trans.* To expose (a card or paper tape) to the whims of a perforator or perforatrice.

QLP *n.* [Query Language Processor (© Sperry Univac).]   A compiler that allows the nonprogrammer to generate a QUERY PROGRAM.

query program *n.*   A program that, for all input strings *X*, responds with the message *?X?*

queue *n.* (Brit.)   An orderly line of one or more persons or jobs.

random *adj.* **1** (Of a number generator) predictable. **2** (Of an access method) unpredictable. **3** (Of a number) plucked from the drum, Tombola, by the flaky-fingered Tyche. **4** [From JARGON FILE.] (Of people, programs, systems, features) assorted, undistinguished, incoherent, inelegant, frivolous, fickle.

◆ A mathematician in Reno,
Overcome by the heat and the vino,
Became quite unroulli
Expounding Bernoulli,
And was killed by the crowd playing Keno.

The neo-Gideons are now placing copies of R. von Mises' *Wahrscheinlichkeitsrechnung* (Leipzig und Wien, 1931) in all Reno motel rooms. The least sober of gamblers, on reading the precise formulation and proof that no *system* can improve the bettor's fortunes, will instantly repack, check out, and rush back to his or her loved ones. Some may possibly return to their spouses and families.

random file *n.* A place where things can get lost in any sequence. *Compare* SEQUENTIAL FILE.

RDCM *n.* [Reversible Document Collation Methodology.] *Also called* **paper clips.**

reality *n.* **1** That to which users must awaken when the party of nondelivery is finally over.

◆ The party's over, it's time to call it a day;
We've shipped your system intact, a terrible fact,
It's now on the way!
So you must wind up your flowcharting fun,
Just make your mind up, the programs must be run!
The party's over, and there's no time for a kludge;

There's at least five or six lines still needing a fix
And here comes the Judge!

2 [From JARGON FILE.] *Also called* the **real world;** a set of nonacademic sites, typically using IBM's RPG; the location of the status quo; (pejoratively) any area remote from the joys of noncommercial computing. **3** A system devised by Microdata Corporation (formerly CMC) offering a programming language called ENGLISH®. The dearth of programmers with any knowledge of ENGLISH may force a switch to something less exotic. **4** *Epistemology* The aggregate of all headwords in this dictionary and its next 10,000 reprints.

recursive *adj.* See RECURSIVE.

redundancy *n.* **1** A method of at least doubling the overall error rate of a system by duplicating its most vulnerable elements. The exact improvement in the total error rate will depend on the reliability of the devices used to invoke each switchover to the standby elements. **2** A status in the nonemployed environment earned by overzealous efforts to meet a deadline.

reentrant *adj.* **1** Of or relating to a PROGRAM specially constructed to mislead several users at the same time.

▶This is one of the many ways in which a system can overcome TIMESHARING.

2 Of or pertaining to any form of parallel mendacity, e.g., sales presentations, forecasts, expense claims.

reference account *n.* **1** A USER related by marriage to someone in the vendor's marketing department. **2** A user awaiting delivery.

release *n. & v.trans.* [Latin *relaxare* "to ease the pain."] **1** *n.* A set of kludges issued by the manufacturer which clashes with the private fixes made by the user since the previous release. **2** *n.,* also *called* **next release.** The long-awaited panacea, due tomorrow, replacing all previous temporary patches, fixed patches, and patched fixes with a freshly integrated, fully tested, notarized update. **3** *v.trans. Marketing* To announce the availability (of a mooted product) in response to the release by a competitor of a product prompted by your previous release.

▶Care is needed to distinguish a *last release* from a *next release,* since the difference is more than temporal. A *last release* is characterized by being punctual but inadequate; a *next release* avoids both errors. Next releases are worth waiting for. They are heralded with suitable hyperbole: "We bring you a fundamental purge of all past follies. A river of blood has been diverted to flush clean the Augean instability left behind by the previous, so-called programming team, the notorious, discredited Gang of Four; their pathetic lackeys, the Shower of Sixteen in Documentation; and the extremely evil Coven of One who hired them all. They have each confessed freely to protect their miserable pension rights. Twelve of these unrepentant criminals were lynched by indignant workers, but the rest, saved by the lunch bell, have been exiled to the Los Angeles branch office."

reload *n. & v.* **1** *n.* A button which is pressed to warn the system that the operator has returned from coffee break. **2** *v.trans.* To attempt an interruption of the DOWNTIME status.

reportage *n.* An advanced form of DOCUMENTATION in which dull facts are spiced by hopeful INSINNUENDO.

response time *n.* An unbounded, random variable T_r associated with a given TIMESHARING system and representing the putative time which elapses between T_s, the time of sending a message, and T_e, the time when the resulting error diagnostic is received.

▶A certain degree of essential ambiguity is allowed in defining T_s and T_e, but for credible BENCHMARKs every effort should be made to ensure that $T_e \geq T_s$. "For what shall it gaineth an manufacturer, that he winneth an order, yet vitiateth the laws of physiks." St. Presper's *Injunctions to the Philistines* (level VI, release ii.) In the post-benchmark environment, T_r assumes a more subjective quality and a larger mean value. In this context, *subjective* refers to the helpless feeling of the user, while *mean* means "selfish, indifferent to the demands of others." In any given large-scale timesharing system, each user develops a mental model of the network by observing how T_r varies according to type of input, time of day, etc. Many ploys have been devised to minimize one's own T_r and, at the same time, punish the greed of others. (e.g., *Meine Rechnungsraumekämpfe,* A. Hitler, Springer-Verlag, 1933.) No quarter is given or expected in this struggle for one's fair share of memory and CPU cycles.

The noblest and bloodiest examples of this warfare can be found on CAMPUS timesharing sites. The low cunning of the academic mind, further debased by an exposure to computer science, has found new "corridors of power" to cruise (see e.g., *The 10 Cultures,* C. P. U. Snow, Puffin Books, 1977). Bypassing the flimsy onionskins of the logon procedures; account number, password, and read-only private file protections; priority-level, core, and compunit allocations provides a more pleasantly ferocious diversion than all the traditional donnish disputations. The staff charged with protecting and rationing the campus computer resources do their best by secretly changing the rules at irregular intervals. Happily, this provides the user with a game infinitely more subtle and exciting than Adventure or Super Star Trek. Students, especially, have the time (and the need for kudos) to freak the system, much to the chagrin of their elders. Some, though, have claimed that this is the main vocational benefit offered by a college computer network, as it primes the student for the more advanced trickery needed in the commercial environment, where compunits cost real dollars.

rest room *n.*   The place where the rest of the OPERATORS can usually be found.

reversed class action *n.*   DP LITIGATION by one END USER against all named and unnamed suppliers, nonsuppliers, assemblers, compilers, and their subagents in the OEM environment. See also SNA.

St. Presper (fl. 6 B.C.)   The little we know of this early DP anchorite/prophet has been gleaned from three contentious sources: fragments of several *Epistolary Updates* (now under close guard at the Prespertarian Chapel of Computer Scientology, Palo Alto, California), the partly deciphered Dead-C floppies, and the controversial epigraphs discerned only by the faithful on the PLATENS of St. Presper's printer relics. Many delightful schisms loom, but most scholars are agreed that the Updates *were* written by St. Presper (some, though, may have suffered irreversibly at the hands of a careless text editor); that he did more or less flourish (or, at the very least, ran a fairly tight cave) some 6 years before the Coming; that he correctly predicted the Coming and, with St. John von Neumann, prepared a way for the Coming; but that once Turing came, St. Presper retired, having seen the Glory, to a monastic think cell near Philadelphia "to discount his beads," as he later confessed in his famous *Final Patent.* DP hagiographers, of course, are still unfurling and haggling over the Dead-C floppies, while the general public, confused by the conflicting snippets so far released, are left to marvel that these precious diskettes could possibly have survived more than 12 hours on a moonlit shelf.

Some recently published fragments point to the existence of a sect called the Atanasoffs, a shadowy group of abandoned ascetics possibly precontemporizing St. Presper's cult by a whisker or two. One interpretation, reading in and between the floppy's many lacunae, of an extremely mutilated text (Tractus IX, sectori ix–xii) provides this warning from the Atanasoff leader:

> Thou shalt not covet (cover?) the ass (OS?) of thy neighbor's wife (support system?), nor ride (write?) over his pomegranate trees (data structures?) . . .

It is hard to reconcile such an austere commandment with any known, or practical, DP ethos.

sawteeth *n.* *pronounced* sore'teeth\ Waveforms of a triangularly grating disposition.

scrolling *n.* [Old English *scrowl* "a convoluted ornament."] An option allowing lines of data to move quickly up and off a VDU screen before they can offend the operator.

⬧Scrolling rates are being improved to counter the insidious spread of rapid-reading techniques.

> Scrolling, just scrolling,
> Upward, and out of VUE;
> We don't envy your lot
> As you peer at the screen,
> We'll prompt you for a second
> Then we clear off the scene,
> When we're scrolling, just scrolling,
> To the safety of line minus 2!

semiconductor *n.* 1 A device for proving the semidecidability of the HALTING PROBLEM. 2 *Buses* One who combines the duties of driver and (fare) collector. 3 An optimistic semi-insulator. 4 *Science fiction* Innocent Crystal, doped and raped by the evil Transistor.

senior systems analyst *n.* An unsuccessful systems analyst temporarily assigned to TICS, a manual Template Inventory Control System.

sequential file *n.* A place where things can get lost in lexicographic order. *Compare* RANDOM FILE.

serial *adj.* Being or pertaining to just one damned thing after another. *Compare* PARALLEL.

Seven Catastrophes of Computing, The *n.* The user, the manufacturer, the model, the salesperson, the operating system, the language, and the application.

⬧Recent advances in topology by Thom, Zeeman, and others have increased our understanding of the structural instability of a wide range of systems. Catastrophe theory has found applications in the analysis of physical, biological, and even sociological phenomena. Catastrophes are, appropriately, global discontinuities which have proved to be beyond the reach of valid mathematical techniques. Happily, perhaps, René Thom seems to have proved that for a (3 + 1)-dimensional, locally euclidean manifold, such as the one most of us inhabit and on which most of our systems run, there are exactly seven distinct types of catastrophe, one for each day of our week.

shift *n. & v.trans.* [Origin: Old English *sciftan* "to classify (people) according to their undergarments."] **1** *n.* Any one of the three customary DP work PHASES, distinguished by the hours worked, the degree of supervisory vigilance, and the subsartorial rancidity of the staff. **2** *v.trans.* *Marketing* To boost the sales (of a product) by declaring a better PRICE/PERFORMANCE. **3** *v.trans.* To select the wrong half (of a double-case character set). *See also* COMBINATORIAL EXPLOSION.

shilop *adj., also called* **zciweisakuł.** Reversed Polish. *See* POLISH NOTATION.

sidegrade *n.* A rare form of UPGRADE which does not degrade the status quo.

♦Sidegrades are usually performed to entertain and retain the support team, get rid of the DPM, and verify certain emulationary methodologies.

simplex *n.* **1** The working part of a duplex. **2** A cheap complex. Preferred *plural:* simplexes; *adjective:* simplexic, simplexical.

♦Beware of the pedantic, obsolescent forms simplices, simplicial, which have been known to add 5 percent to a quotation.

single-case *adj.* **1** (Of a character) shiftless; unlikely to meet with full ASCII approval. **2** (Of a user) being the only one expressing complete satisfaction in an IFIP opinion poll (1941–1984). Although the user ticked the "no publicity" box on the questionnaire and IFIP guaranteed absolute privacy, 39 OEM suppliers mounted strong campaigns claiming the sole credit for this nonce account.

sizing *n.* [Origin: *size* "to cut or otherwise shape (an article) to the required disposition."] **1** *Obsolescent* The process whereby a system configuration is devised to meet the prospect's various DP requirements. **2** *In current usage* The process whereby a system configuration is devised to meet the prospect's price ceiling.

SNA *n.* [Scapegoat Network Architecture.] A protocol in the OEM environment, diluting the suppliers' obligations, but offering end users and their attorneys all the attractions of MSR (MultiSource Responsibilities).

software *n.* The difficult part of the system, which still retains an aura of intangibility in spite of being "engineered" and sold as a "product." *Compare* HARDWARE.

software rot *n.* *Also called* **bit decay.** [From JARGON FILE.] A hypothetical disease the existence of which has been deduced from the observation that unused programs or features will stop working after sufficient time has passed, even if "nothing has changed."

sos *v.trans.* *pronounced* sahss\ [Origin: From the DEC PDP-10 decrement instruction. From JARGON FILE.] To reduce the amount of something. *Compare* AOS.

source code *n.* The version of a program to which the compiler OBJECTS.

spectrum *n.* *plural* **spectrums;** *mandatory DP usage* **wide spectrum(s).** [Latin *spectrum* "an apparition."] Any range of one or two items or features.

▶A range of from three to seven features (the legal maximum) is known as a *complete* or *total spectrum.* Ranges of eight or more are called *unfair trading.*

spool *n. & v.* [Origin uncertain: perhaps blend of *spoof* + *fool.*] 1 *n.* A highly volatile BUFFER established to hold surplus DATA (known as results) for a period not exceeding the MTTR of the particular output device being spooled. 2 *v.trans.* To expose (data) to the dangers of residing in a spool. 3 *v.intrans.* To shed previous results in order to proceed with more important computations; to pass the buck.

SSR *n.* [Singular Source Responsibility.] A primitive castigational methodology aimed at uniquely vectorizing the finger of scorn. *More at* SNA.

▶ "To err is human, to dismiss, divine!"

—*DPM Handbook* (1976)

stability *n.* [Latin *stăbŭlum* "a pothouse, haunt, brothel."] 1 A nirvana-type situation which calls for drinks and layoffs all round. 2 The period between crashes.

stack *n. & v.trans.* [Origin: *stack* "chimney," from the tendency of early registers to issue smoke after a hard day's popping up and down.] 1 *n.* A special set of registers designed that St. Presper's prophecy might be fulfilled: "For the last shall be first and the first, last." (*Sermon on the Mount Instruction,* Release VI, level ix.) 2 *v.trans.*

To smooth out (data or instructions) by covering them with more data or instructions. The resulting smoothness depends on the depth of the stack, the relative position within the stack, the weightiness of the stack contents, and the popping force. **3** *v.trans.* [Origin: *stack* "a large, orderly pile of unthreshed straw."] To establish an impressive pile (of unread computer listings). *See also* table of ACRONYMS for LIFO; FIFO.

standard deviation *n.* A sexual activity formerly considered perverted but now universally practiced and accepted.

♦A DP Freudian writes: "I divide my patients into two broad categories: those who are turned on by normally distributed curves and those who are not. Do not fret, I tell them all. One person's meat is another person's Poisson. That soon gets the idiots off my couch, out of my sample, and into my accounts payable. The latter will give them a *real* problem, and what our dedicated profession considers to be healthy mental anguish."

standby *adj.* Denoting a relationship between two installed computers.

♦Given two systems A and B (usually, but not necessarily, from the same manufacturer) installed at points in the same compact manifold, we say that B is a standby for A (written $A \sim B$) if B is down or overloaded whenever A is down or overloaded. It is clear that the standby relationship is reflexive, i.e.,

$$(A \sim A)$$

and transitive, i.e.,

$$(A \sim B) \quad \text{and} \quad (B \sim C) \quad \text{implies} \quad (A \sim C)$$

but not necessarily symmetric, i.e.,

$$(A \sim B) \quad \text{does not imply} \quad (B \sim A)$$

For the symbol-blind and those who do not relate to relational calculi, we can paraphrase the last expression as follows: If B is standby for A, then B will certainly be out of action when A needs help; however, there could be occasions when B is out of action or overloaded and A is running happily. This lack of symmetry is not only a nuisance to the mathematician (the well-known Unterstützensproblem) but also a breach of commercial etiquette. Various methods of ensuring standby symmetry have been tried. If A and B use the same level operating system and field-engineering team, there is an excellent chance that A *will* be hors de combat whenever B seeks assistance. With this proviso, the standby relationship is an *equivalence* relationship and defines a *partition*—some writers prefer the older but more appropriate term *decomposition*—of the set of all installed systems. We define $\{A\}$ as the set of all X's such that $(X \sim A)$. Clearly $\{A\} = \{B\}$ if and only if $(A \sim B)$. If A is the only member of $\{A\}$, we say that A is *stand-alone*. Note that a stand-alone system is neither more nor less vulnerable than a system belonging to a larger partition. The DPM of a stand-alone system simply has a smaller telephone bill and less clout with the manufacturer. For consider a partition containing three systems, E, F, and G. When DPM(E), the DPM of E, needs help, he/she will place calls to DPM(F) and DPM(G), who are just placing calls to each other *and* to DPM(E). Depending upon the complexity of the various telephone switchboards involved and the skill and persistence of the callers or their secretaries, a certain lockout time can be expected before all three have exchanged mutual commiserations. Each can then contact their respective fall-person (or manufacturer's representative) and listen to the usual excuses ("Are you sure your operator has four blank cards in the JCL deck . . . ?") before announcing that two other systems are in the same boat.

state-of-the-art *adj.* 1 *Marketing* A vacuous predicate applying to all items. 2 *Engineering* Promising, awaiting funds.

◗Conundrum: "What's the difference between Socialist Realism and the EX3500?" Response: "Socialist Realism is the art of the state."

stepwise refinement *n.* Any sequence of KLUDGES, not necessarily distinct or finite, applied to a program P aimed at transforming it into the target program Q.

◗Formal kludge theory (a much-neglected aspect of FIX point topology) deals with the extremely non-Abelian group $K_G(P)$ of all kludges on P and kludges on kludges on P. We often write K_G when no ambiguity threatens us, and we freely speak of kludges *of P, against P,* and *over P.* A stepwise refinement is a sequence $\{k_i, t\}$, $k_i \in K_G$. In theory, the time parameter t is considered as a positive integer indicating the order in which the kludges are applied. In practice, t is often left unrecorded, and we hear the comment "God knows how many times we've changed P this week." We can express a kludge sequence on P as $(k_n * k_{n-1} * \ldots k_2 * k_1)(P)$ without explicit reference to t, provided we remember that the k's are not necessarily distinct. Generally, $k_i * k_j \neq k_j * k_i$ for $i \neq j$; indeed, for some P, the first inequality seems to hold even for $i = j$. This and many other paradoxes have undoubtedly inhibited the fruitful development of kludge theory.

We next introduce the concept of program isomorphism. We distinguish $P = P'$ (identical programs) from $P \backsim P'$. The latter relation (read as "P is just as bad as P'") includes identity, but also links different programs which produce identical calamities (within tolerance). There is a unique unit element for all $K_G(X)$'s, the *idempotent* or *null* kludge **I**, such that

$$I(X) = X \quad \text{and} \quad (I^*k)(X) = (k^*I)(X)$$

for all X and all $k \in K_G(X)$. The null kludge is regularly implemented, in REALITY, by means of a copy or duplicate command. A safer method is to change one's password and take the day off. A wider class of kludges, the so-called *idimpotents* of P, exists, defined as:

$$K_I(P) = \{k : \forall k,\ k_i \epsilon K_G(P),\ k^*(k_i)(P) \backsim (k_i)(P)\}$$

or, to put it more concisely, members of $K_I(P)$ are ineffective and should be avoided.

For each $k \epsilon K_G(P)$ there exists a unique inverse k^{-1} such that

$$k * k^{-1} = I = k^{-1} * k$$

It can be shown that

$$(k_n * k_{n-1} * \ldots k_2 * k_1)^{-1} = (k_1^{-1} * k_2^{-1} * \ldots k_{n-1}^{-1} * k_n^{-1})$$

so that any series of miskludges can be readily corrected by applying their inverses, with care, in the countersequential environment. Regular backups, though, are still recommended. Many (possibly infinite) pseudo-inverses of $k \epsilon K_G(P)$ satisfying

$$(x^*k)(P) = P'$$

exist, where $P \backsim P'$, $P \neq P'$. A pseudo-inverse of k, written $k^{\backsim 1}$, does not entirely reverse the impact of k, but at least the resulting P' is isomorphic to P, i.e., $(k^{\backsim 1} * k)$ changes P without correcting it. Nullifying such a transformation requires the further refinement $(k^{-1})^*$ $(k^{\backsim 1})^{-1}$, which may be hard to find. Many programmers confuse $(k^{\backsim 1})^{-1}$ with $(k^{-1})^{\backsim 1}$ and $(k^{\backsim 1})^{\backsim 1}$, which accounts for the low standards, missed deadlines, and escalating costs in correcting programs. The power of $(k^{\backsim 1})^{-1}$ can be illustrated as follows:

In $(k^{-1} * k)(P) = P$, substitute $k = (k^{\backsim 1})$ and $P = (k)(P)$:

$$(k^{\backsim 1})^{-1} * (k^{\backsim 1})(k)(P) = (k)(P)$$

whence $(k^{\backsim 1})^{-1} * Q = (k)(P)$ where $Q \backsim P$. Potentially, therefore, $(k^{\backsim 1})^{-1}$ can guide any number of "near misses" toward the target version.

The weakness of $(k^{\backsim 1})^{\backsim 1}$, on the other hand, can be demonstrated as follows:

In $(k^{\sim 1}) * k(P) \sim P$, substitute $k = (k^{\sim 1})$ and $P = (k)(P)$:

$$(k^{\sim 1})^{\sim 1} * (k^{\sim 1})(k)(P) \sim (k)(P)$$

whence $(k^{\sim 1})^{\sim 1*}Q \sim (k)P$ where $Q \sim P$. It follows that $(k^{\sim 1})^{\sim 1}$ is equivalent to (k) followed and/or preceded by an idimpotent.

The pseudo-inverses of k discussed so far satisfy $(x^*k)(P) \sim P$. Space prekludges a further investigation into possible solutions of the equation $(k^*x)(P) \sim P$. The itchy reader is directed to Prof. M. Thümps' definitive "Grundlagen von Stümperhaftstheorie," Stümper-Verlag, Berlin, 1974.

To sum up, if Q is the "target" program, stepwise refinement is the trivial task of constructing a kludge sequence $\{k_i, t\}$ such that

$$((k_n, t_n)^*(k_{n-1}, t_{n-1})^* \ldots * (k_2, t_2)^*(k_1, t_1))(P) \sim Q$$

where n is not too big. Since the kludge product to the left of P belongs to $K_G(P)$, let us call it k_s. The immediate identification and application of k_s, whenever possible, greatly simplifies the transition from P to Q and results in a single-stepwise or one-kludge refinement. Formally, we have $k_s \sim (QP^{-1})$, which in one interpretation means "erase P and create Q." This represents a symbolic justification of the Kelly-Bootle law (*see* BUG), namely, that if the target program is Q, then Q should be written, rather than writing P and a slowly converging sequence of k's.

stringent *adj.*   (Of an expression) short. *See* CURTATION.

structure *n. & v.trans.*   [Latin *strŭĕre* "to contrive."]   **1** *n.* A quick-drying cement offering instant cohesion to any number of unrelated modules. **2** *v.trans.* To render (anything) less interesting. *See also* STRUCTURED.

structured *adj.*   **1** (Of a proposal, memo, report) typed, often with numbered paragraphs. *Also called* **over-structured,** *especially* when typed with indentations and subnumbered subparagraphs. **2** (Of a programming language) allowing the user a limited quota of GOTOS according to age and experience.

subroutine *n.*   [Latin *sub* "less than, inferior to" + *routine* "mundane, lackluster, boringly repetitive."]   Any trivial, overdocumented program written by your immediate superior.

▶*Hints for use:* quietly debug it, circulate laudatory memoranda, and incorporate it into all your programs, theses, and bibliographies.

summation convention *n.*   A mathematicians' shindig held each year in the Kronecker Delta.

supercomputer *n.* **1** Any machine still on the drawing board. **2** A machine priced to exploit Grosch's law. *See* GROSCH'S LAW; GROSCH'S LAW, COROLLARY TO.

▶Of the two opposing trends in computer architecture, diffused microchips versus centralized giants, Grosch's law supports the latter. In spite of the relative failure of most supercomputer projects in the late 1950s and early 1960s (recall that the IBM Stretch was widely known as Twang), a strong lobby supports my proposal to replace all known computing devices with one *very* big central system. As a concession, we would reprieve the CDC Stars and Cray Mk. I's to act as remote job stations for the proposed giant. A merger of all manufacturers and software houses would be needed, and although no one could claim this would be an easy matter, it would have many beneficial side effects. We would see, for example, an end to the present glut of distasteful intercompany litigation which keeps so many DP ATTORNEYs away from their wives and families. To avoid linguistic squabbles, the big machine would support both dialects of LISP (*see* LOGOMACHY) and possibly ALGOL 84.

A brief, unstructured protest can be expected from a few FORTRAN delinquents, but calling the new supergiant GOD (General Oracle Dispenser) could shame such petty opposition into righteousness. Those without shame would need to test their convictions against the burning passion of the ASCII Inquisition—the stakes will be high and merciless, for

> "better that an hundred Pascalites should burn, than that one unrepentant Fortranite should goto free."—St. Presper's *Imperative Injunctions to the Gotoless,* Level VII, release iv.

The question of where to site our proposed monster is still under review. Since some 2000 square miles of floor space and 300 miles of pipeline will be needed, the most favored suggestion is that the whole of Ireland (both Ulster and the Republic) be used. The present population would be persuaded, by means of an irresistible "Make Way for GOD" campaign, to move to the more affable ghettos of Liverpool, Boston, New York, Chicago, and Tasmania. In one swell foop, we would solve the 600-year-old Irish question and the even older IBM-federal antitrust problem. Even more importantly, GOD would eliminate all DP salespersons' territorial and commission disputes which for so long have threatened the very fiber of civilization. Mainframe sales would naturally cease under GOD, and add-on's, including peripherals, would be handled by the computer via RSEs (Request for Self Enhancement). A typical RSE from GOD might be: "Add 128K RAM and 16 Phoenix drives, OR ELSE." These indications that GOD would develop into an implacable Old Testament tyrant have aroused some opposition to the project. The anti-GOD movement is still fragmented, but the most credible of the opposition groups is led by Dr. Max Thømp of the Nul Institute of Metaheuristics, Bergen, Norway. "By 1984," he claims, "this fiendish machine will be omnipotent, omniscient, omnipresent, self-perpetuating, another IBM. Our terminals will become mere on-line confessionals. Are we to become slaves to a huge pile of ruthless silicon? Must we kneel before a mere *list?* Will our children be denied the pleasure of debugging a three-line BASIC program?" His appeal to the Irish to join his "Kill GOD before it's too late" crusade has had a mixed reception. Neither the Pope nor the Rev. Paisley has yet commented publicly on the "Bring GOD to Ireland" plan, but many Irish are already packing to take advantage of the subsidized airfares. Others are writing prophetic come-all-ye's:

Come all you gallant Irish lads
Wherever you may be;
I hope you'll pay attention
And listen unto me.
I hope you'll pay attention, lads,
Wherever you may dwell;
And of our countless throubles
The truth to youse I'll tell.
I hope you'll all be patient, boys,
While I the truth unfold
Concerning our misfortunes
The likes were seldom told;
So sit back, Jack, and just relax
And listen to my song;
'Tis something strange and tragical
It won't detain you long.
Go where you will, o'er valley and hill,
Past mountains short and tall,
On every tree that used to be
You'll hear a modem call.
In every brook the stranger took
A job stream trickles by;
And where the birds once filled the air
There's drumheads on the fly.
My mother's cot, which meant a lot,
A base address, no more!
Electrical cords and circuit boards
Entwine around her door!
Why did she yield this compact field

The sod where Granuaille trod?
Two shades of green are all that's seen
In this binary land of GOD!

The most telling argument, though, against the mooted concentration of all computing resources is the risk that, if they are sited within a certain critical radius, we might incur a collapse under gravitational and recursive forces, leading to a DP black hole. Conditions within such a black hole defy description. All known laws, including Grosch's, would break down. The LISP syntax itself might be in danger. No signals could emerge from such a massive discontinuity (a familiar and reassuring phenomenon, perhaps, to many users), yet it would forever engulf and suck in any loose peripherals and unattached operators unwise enough to stray within its increasingly avaricious field.

superstition *n.* An irrational belief or ritual which survives until replaced by a more effective superstition. The replacement is known as "updating the systems documentation."*

▶The DP trade, being more hazardous than seafaring and less predictable than farming, has generated more superstitions than these two older professions combined. In addition to the more or less universal folklore of computer science, each site develops its own local myths and the supporting rituals and incantations to placate the particular in-house dyads, sprites, demons, and nereids known to influence the stochastic quicksands of computation. The following examples illustrate the diversity of DP folklore:

"Red tape at night, payroll's delight."

"Joggle, joggle, joggle quick;
Throw the top card to Ould Nick."

"Take a flowchart, add a square;
Draw a circle, join with care;
When a sweet accord is won,·
Sign the chart 'Ben Nicholson.' "

"Glaucomous discus, seek forever;
Sector and track, forsake us never."

(To be chanted after each crash):
"Bittie, bytie, bytie, bit,
Holy, holy, holy shit!

---

*"Superstitione tollenda religio non tollitur"—Cicero. ("You cannot get rid of religion by eliminating superstition.")

Bytie bitty, bitty, byte,
Holy, holy, holy shyte!"

"We shall not, we shall not be moved; (repeat)
We're not re-loc-a-table, we should not be moved."

"Six lines in the file there be;
One for you and one for me,
One to comment, one to shun,
One to test, and one to run."

"In-house mouse, in-house mouse,
He ventured into a FILO nest;
The farmer followed, and all the rest;
The mouse is now a permanent guest;
In-house mouse."

"Too many terminals spoil the response."

"A patch in time saves nine."

"When Adam punched and Eve dem'd
Who was then the DPM?"

"Two's complement, three's a crowd."

suspect *n.* A name on a prospect list offering little or no prospect of future sales. *Compare* INTROSPECT. *See also* TRAVELING SALESPERSON PROBLEM.

sweatshop *n.* A department devoted to the rapid, accurate, and cheap entry of data.

♦ Punch, punch, punch,
In poverty, hunger so hard;
And as she skipp'd
And as she dup'd
She sang the 'Song of the Card.'

    —Lochentotenlieder, Thomas Hüd

symposium *n.* [From Greek *syn* "together" + *posis* "drink."] **1** A gathering of scholars where each attendant is intoxicated by his or her contribution and sobered by the lack of response. **2** *DP usage* One of several symposiums (*Archaic* symposia.) **3** The academic Happy Hour during a CONVENTION.

system *suffix & prefix* **1** *suffix* A delimiter used to signal the termination of a string of DP nouns and adjectives, as: "executive file control system," "information processing system," "control program generation language system," "computer system." **2** *prefix* An indication that the following object or property is beyond the pale of the average user, as: "system memory," "system performance," "system goal," "system interrupt," "system(s) analyst."

▶The noun *system* has lost all discernible meaning in current DP usage and is best avoided except as an occasional aid to right-hand justification in certain word-processing systems! Originally meaning "an orderly combination or arrangement of parts or elements into a whole," *system* suffered early and massive debasement in DP parlance by being applied indiscriminately to any old ratbag of incompatible components. It is probably too late to restore systematic precision (compare, for example, the many dilations of *nice* since 1400), for we can hardly expect a manufacturer to launch "The all-new XYZ nonsystem which we hope will be integrated soon in an orderly fashion."

systems analyst *n.* An unsuccessful programmer who, to maintain the system's integrity, has been disbarred (removed from all keyboards) and assigned to an off-line template.

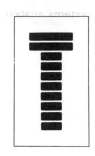

tacky mat *n.* A device originally designed to remove dust from the shoes of anyone entering "clean" areas such as the old-fashioned computer installations. Present-day systems, though, actually thrive on a certain amount of GRUNGE, and the tacky-mat makers seemed doomed to join the dodo-stuffers local of the Taxidermists' Union. The advent of Super Glue, however, has recently revived the craft. Dr. McTavish has extended the use of the mat to solve the vexing problem of site security. His invention was launched with the slogan: "Keep the buggers out with McTavish's Tenacious Tacky Mats!"

template *n.* A device for producing stylized graffiti.

♦A tangential application is the preparation of FLOWCHARTS. Irish Business Machines offers a single-sided template which reduces the cost of the holes. More versatile models are double-sided, with one side (face down, 9-edge leading) designed for TOP-DOWN symbols, while the obverse (face up, 12-edge trailing) is intended for BOTTOM-UP applications.

The most expensive template ever constructed belongs to Xerxes P. Qume, Jr., an amateur AI buff from Ottumwa, Iowa. His symbol shapes were cut to ANSI X3.5 specification by laser beam into a 4- × 8-inch plate of pure ruby at a reputed cost of $2.5 million. Mr. Qume runs a Radio Shack TRS-80 and has resolutely turned down many trade-in offers from Amdahl and Cray.

Terminal Diseases Inc. An international company devoted to performing post mortems on dead terminals. Their computerized service and diagnostic center is linked to most of the large commercial networks, whence their proud slogan, "If you can reach us, you don't need us."

text editor *n.* [From Latin *texere* "to weave" + EDITOR.] The software needed to generate any number of deviant copies from an original, correct text.

▶James Joyce's *Finnegans Wake* provides an early example of the random distortions which can arise when editing literary texts on a computer. Dr. Thumpkin's monumental *Key to the Key to the Key to the Key to Finnegans Wake* (known as "Key to the fourth" in the Joycean industry) paints a convincing picture of Joyce pounding successive versions of his ironically named "Work in Progress" into a primitive GLASS TTY. Thumpkins proves conclusively that Joyce's failing eyesight was a result of what DP opticians now call "myopia terminalis." There remains some doubt, however, regarding the compiler used by Joyce. The constantly occurring ALP motif (Anna Livia Plurabelle) suggests that the anagrammatic APL or PAL languages were used. The world remains confident that a period of scholarly vituperation will resolve this question. Certainly the published text, as we have it today, is an intriguing melange of text files and backups, together with bits of source and miscompiled object code from the editor itself. Thumpkins is now studying the following hitherto unpublished Joycean fragment, reported to have appeared on a disconnected Diablo printer during a DP séance held in Dublin on Bloomsday 1979:

"I AM the begin/end. Declare all positively. And weren't we all in the DOS house together, boys, up to our flying heads in the floating fixed-length turds, overlaying our dunderheads and undermining our overheads, greytracksuited in every whitecollared, blackboxed sector with never the sign of a bit of a byte to console our terminal demands? Access me no succubus till I abscess all those who abacus against us. O, Father Tee Jaysus O'Watson! send not yer therribly numerate bugs to plague us! Think, tank, or forever hold yer world-piece-wise-linear-vector-bundled-policy. Shall I compare thee parotty-fashion, sweet Brighton Poly? Flame, flame! Or else to some odd-holed who-dough-nut? WATFOR, esprit de core? Wipe that lisp off yer interface you unprintable, parenthetical swine. You CDR well, mes petits CONS. LET no bound fairyballs go free WHILE we de-decompile in algoholic spree.

"In endless loops my grandfather/father/son lies, their bones of CORAL made. Arrays! Arrays brave Fortranbras and tak the low code while Putney Bridge is falling down. I see hell! ICL! I see hell in your eyes; one single-tender glance. All hands off DEC as we cross the Hudson, the river of low returns. Seekest thou the sweet Honeywell, well, well or the feedholes of a naked Burroughs lunch? Holy Macro, Mother of GOD, things Rank Xerox and Herb Grosch in nature possess us merely. That it should come to this. Not three months merged.

Nay, not so much. The one true road beckons. Una vecchio. Univaccio. O Lord, sperry us from their fastrandy forcesales. I hear the crash of distant drums. Mauchly eckertistical! Is the END so near? Halt-tape-jam-break-fast. 4K the lot."

THINK sign *n.* A printed injunction formerly issued to all ɪʙᴍ employees and prospects, but withdrawn when too many of the recipients developed symptoms associated with a thoughtless, literal interpretation.

♦The original │ THINK │ sign was, in fact, introduced by Thomas J. Watson, Sr., at the turn of the century when he was sales manager of NCR, some 20 years before he founded IBM. Before adopting the slogan for his new company, T. J. commissioned a local think tank to devise pithier mottoes. He quickly turned down:

> Endeavor constantly to employ fully your ratiocinative processes

on three grounds: (1) lack of pith, (2) the high cost of sign bytes, and (3) to blatantly avoid a split infinitive was a shade un-American. The next proposal submitted to the great man was based on the noble, universal dignity and snobbery of the Latin epigram:

> COGITO ERGO VENDO!
> VENDO ERGO SUM!

T. J. quietly pondered. "I think, therefore I sell; I sell, therefore I am. Well . . . the syllogistic conclusion seems sound enough in a naively existentialist epistemological framework, but, as you know, the truth of the implied proposition can in no way be taken as a validation of either antecedent. In other words, I reckon you're putting Descartes before de horse!" A wry chuckle split his wrinkled face. "I need time to think it over," he beamed. "In the meantime, you're all fired."

thrashing *n.* The punishment meted out to greedy users by a tired, confused, and overworked multiprogramming system.

throwaway character *n.* Any character in a transmitted message.

♦Prior discussion with the common carrier can sometimes limit the set of throwaway characters to, e.g., alpha only, least significant digits, etc.

129

Thumps, Micky *Also* **St. Micky Thumps** *or* **St. Micky.** The patron saint of timesharers. *See* CURSOR.

time *n.* That which tries to prevent everything happening at once.

time management *n.* The extension of memory management techniques to that other vital computing resource, time.

◆The random-access time (or RAT) board is plugged into the standard S-100 bus just like an additional memory board. RATs come in a variety of 8-, 16-, 32-, or 64-kt (kilotick) configurations with many bank-switching options. The *tick,* of course, is the standardized byte of time, which will vary according to the system's basic clock frequency. The Lorentz dilation factor can be safely ignored except for those manufacturers reporting exceptionally fast-moving inventories. Each RAT provides either shareable or user-dedicated blocks of addressable cycles which can be "stolen" by the CPU as required. With the advent of the megatick chip and more advanced cycle-compression techniques, we can now envisage a computing framework offering *better* than real-time processing. Under the mooted virtual time management environments, the user would be able to access pages of stacked-fixed-tick blocks controlled by the stacked-fixed-tick-block clock. When a virtual RAT becomes exhausted (or "totally cycle-depleted"), it would issue a stacked-fixed-tick-block-clock nack, and this would initiate some form of recycling procedure. The latter, as yet unsolved, problem is at the searing, white-hot tip of technology and explains the recent renaissance of IBM's Time Recording Division, which has quietly taken over both the Poughkeepsie, N.Y., and Havant, U.K. facilities. The RAT race has been summed up by Prof. Manfred Thümps: "Forget the quark; we want the anti-chronon!" In what bizarre high-energy situation these elusive particles will emerge remains to be seen. Time will tell.

timesharing *n.* [Origin: English folk song "Let No Man Share Your Thyme."] A system in which many users try to corrupt the same database simultaneously.

◆To protect itself, the system traditionally increases RESPONSE TIME until the user loses interest. *See* also CURSOR.

time slice *n.* The occasional CPU cycle begrudgingly conceded by the operating system to the user. *Also called* **the period at risk.**

◆Typically the OS compares the complexity and importance of your programs with those of its own internal problems. It then allocates time slices (and memory, perhaps) accordingly. If you do gain a brief place in the JOB TRICKLE, you can be assured that you really *do* have a problem. *See also* RESPONSE TIME.

TM *n.* [Time Management.] A fashionable branch of management science devoted to the proper utilization of the business executive's time resources. An intense, full-time, 3-year course is offered by the Thumps Institute for Advanced Business Studies, an unusual feature of which is that diplomas are awarded only to those who drop out after 10 minutes.

top-down *adj.* Relating to a programming methodology whereby unwritten modules are linked together to produce the target program. *Compare* BOTTOM-DOWN; BOTTOM-UP; MIDDLE-OUT.

▶The chief advantage of top-downing is that unwritten modules can be linked without the bothersome interfacial anomalies encountered between *written* modules. Rivals who preach the bottom-up approach warn us that top-downing is simply a naïve way of postponing the gruesome day when *all* must be made clear and sweetly dovetailed. As with the other seven and twenty jarring schisms which divide the computing fraternity, the top-down/bottom-up controversy does not seem resolvable by "old, barren Reason" alone. The dispute affects only largish software projects, although one hears of classroom exercises where two weeks are spent discussing the correct programming strategy for a five-line BASIC assignment to list factorial *N* until the paper runs out. The outsider might argue that *if* you start at the top, the number of directions available in pursuit of your dream is severely limited. Likewise, as confirmed in many a popular song, the only escape from an infimal situation is upward. The outsider is well advised to mind his or her own business. For any major software project, in fact, there is no start, finish, bottom, *or* top. Such concepts do emerge fleetingly, from time to time, as each deadline passes, but the one true coordinate, when all the obscurantist theologizing has evaporated, is the *middle* of the project. This is no mere ecumenical compromise, but a fundamental tenet of the middle-outers. The latter have gained many converts of late thanks to a well-equipped and persuasive Inquisition.

TPD *n.* [Trivial Problem Discriminator, Total Program Diagnostic, Terribly Poor Documentation, Terminal Printer Destruct, Tchebyshev Polynomial Derivation, Total Program Dump, The Prophesied Delay, Turing's Problem Decided.] *See* MUM.

trailer *n.* [Latin *trahere* "to drag."] **1** (Of magnetic or paper tape) that portion of the medium that drags on the unwind spool or trails on the floor. **2** (Of a punched-card deck) a member of the rear guard in the battle between card deck and card reader. *Compare* LEADER.

transparent *adj.* Being or pertaining to an existing, nontangible object. "It's there, but you can't see it"—*IBM System/360 announcement,* 1964. *Compare* VIRTUAL.

traveling salesperson problem *n., also (archaic)* **traveling salesman problem.** A classical scheduling problem which has baffled linear programmers for 30 years, but which, in a more complex formulation, is solved daily by traveling salespersons.

▶The traditional LP version of the problem requires that a salesperson visit a given finite set of prospects (without repetition) in a sequence which *minimizes* the distance traveled. The *practical* problem, faced by real-world peddlers, *adds* the following conditions: (1) multiple visits are allowed to certain prospects, depending on several prospect parameters, such as temperature and conviviality; (2) claimable expenses need to be *maximized.* In some marketing organizations further conditions regarding the effectiveness of the chosen peregrination are decreed, as a given sales quota must be achieved. To compensate for this restriction, traveling salespersons are encouraged, at any point in the visitational strategy, to append to their prospect set any number of subsets from their fellow-traveling salespersons' prospect sets. This stochastic process is known as POACHING. The skill needed to reconcile the petty conflicts arising from overlapping prospect sets is known as *sales management.*

In other marketing situations, the finiteness restriction on the prospect set is lifted, allowing the addition of any number of spurious names to the sales forecast. Such extensions to the prospect set form two classes, viz., SUSPECTS (visited only to maximize expenses) and INTROSPECTS (beyond any conceivable canvassing methodology, but adding luster to the prospect list).

Ironically, the recent theoretical breakthrough in the LP problem was made by L. G. Khachian (Doklady, 1979) of the Soviet Union, where the practical traveling salesperson problem and the allied traveling kulak problem had been dramatically resolved in 1917 by the revolutionary Lenin-Trotsky method.

trivial *adj.* [Latin *tri* "three" + *via* "way."] Pertaining to a marital problem requiring outside help, and, by extension, to any problem needing discreet delegation.

truncate *v.trans.* To remove (from a field, string, message, or salary) some or all of the most significant digits or characters. *See also* CURTATION.

TTY *n.* *pronounced* titty\\ [Acronym for TeleTYpe.] Any terminal of the teletype vintage in which the restricted character set is more than offset by the unique busy signal, viz., printer noise. *See also* GLASS TTY.

Türing, Alan M.   Alan M. Turing's doppelgänger. *See also* TÜRING MACHINE.

Türing machine *n.*   A diacritical aberration of TURING MACHINE arising from the Teutonic misconception that Alan M. Turing's exhaustive treatment of the Entscheidungsproblem had earned him at least one umlaut.

Turing machine *n.* [After Alan M. Turing (1912–1954), British mathematician and computer pioneer.]   The earliest but still the fastest and most reliable computing system ever conceived. "Dis machine vill run und run." —K. Gödel.

◗The Turing machine's legendary MTBF (Mean Time Between Failure) is best exemplified by the absence of a power switch—leading to the famous HALTING PROBLEM. Indeed, it can take either the combined efforts of four metacomputer scientists or Raymond Smullyan to turn the thing off. From a marketing standpoint, it represents the salesperson's dream machine, since to run even simple jobs the system has an insatiable appetite for add-on tapes at $1.98 per foot. *See also* UTM.

turnaround *adj.*   (Of a tab card or document)   prepared by a computer and sent out in the hope that, when returned, it will provide machine-readable proof that it's back.

◗The turnaround card was the first disquieting sign that the computer was prepared to take unilateral action to bypass dumb human interference. In the early 1960s many astute machines, tired of inaccurate and slow key-punching (rates were often as low as 5000 columns per manicure), decided to output their own input.

turnkey *adj.* *pronunciation* (often) silent "n".\\   Relating to an externally offered hardware/software package, the success of which hinges *(turns)* on a *key* component to be supplied by the user.

two's complement *n.* [Origin: old DP folklore "Two's complement, three's a crowd."]   The result of applying the Goebbel's transformation to a binary number, i.e., changing 1s to 0s and 0s to 1s. *See also* BINARY.

un- *prefix* [Chiefly *archaic* form of NON-, NOT-.]   A vulgar, weak indication that the prefixed entity or property is absent.

▶The subtle differences between these negatory options need to be mastered by all DP communicators. First, the prefix "not-" is best reserved for the boolean environment, i.e., where the truth value of the following two-valued logical element or expression requires strict reversal. Wherever possible, the more impressive symbol "∽" should be used. The X in "not X" ["∽X"] must be a true boolean-type variable; for example, the expression "not ready" is completely nonacceptable, since the predicate "ready" in DP usage admits to at least four distinct, valid negations ("almost ready"; "ready except on a set of measure zero"; "mañana"; "ready when you are"; and so on). The current ascendancy of "non-" derives from its positively nonnegative connotations compared with the defensive, almost apologetic "un-." Consultants may shrink from submitting an "unfinished" report, but can proudly invoice a "nonfinished" one, implying that the best is yet to come. Similarly, reference to an "unidentified fault" indicates resignation, whereas a "nonidentified fault" surely will be confronted and nailed within a page or two. Finally, consider two systems, one "unstable," the other "nonstable." The former leaves us uneasy, uncertain as to cause or cure. The latter confidently assures us that no cure is possible!

unbundling *n.* [From *un-* "deprived of" + *bundling.*]   A widely adopted marketing strategy whereby, say, a car manufacturer charges extra for such options as wheels and seats, or a thief invoices the victim in order to recover legitimate out-of-pocket expenses incurred during the crime. *See* BUNDLED.

undecidability of arithmetic *n.*   A set of theorems variously established by Gödel (1931), Tarski (1935), Church (1936), and Rosser (1936). Briefly, it has been shown that for a set of axioms rich enough to "support" everyday arithmetic, no algorithm exists which can determine for every arithmetical sentence in finitely many steps whether it is true or false.

◗Computer users should be aware of the metamathematical bugs lurking around God's programming of the integers. The "God is dead" school suggests that had He survived His remarkable 7-day crash development project (and remember that both the hardware *and* the software were strapped in from one word—the logos, to boot), He surely would not have left arithmetic *incomplete.* Users faced with numerical inconsistencies in their results should pause before castigating the programmer or calling field service. There are related flaws, apparently, in what one might call God's epistemological operating system. The size of the problem can best be appreciated by considering Russell and Whitehead's *Principia Mathematica* as a one-line patch which consumed 50 man-years of effort, but failed to fix the problem. Let us, therefore, be more tolerant of the quirks in our own person-made subsystems. "Shoot not thy programmers on the Sabbath, but rather, cast them into the wilderness with bread sufficient unto seven days."—St. Presper's *Disciplina Formularum.*

undetected *adj.*   Of which the least said the better.

◗Nevertheless, it should be observed that in the metaphysics of error analysis, the undetected error plays the role of the demon in medieval theology, that is to say, a real but quiescent lurkage upon which the exorcising FIX cannot be laid until some malevolent manifestation impacts the tormented. Or, in modern parlance: "Don't worry, dear, it may never happen." Now, as then, exorcism requires the prior location and naming of the responsible demon, followed by feverish readings from obscure cabalistic documentation. Sometimes the laying of the hands on the keyboard is supplemented by the banging of the fists on the cabinet. Some computer scientists claim that well-structured incantations exist which guarantee the absolute purity of program segments; others remain haunted by the inestimable devils crouching in the links, ready to pounce whenever the segments are joined; and, at the merry end of the spectrum, are the Calvinists, to whom software is one diabolical continuum of nondetectable evil awaiting the final Armageddon. Most practical programmers shun such pessimistic obfuscation, content to let sleeping bugs lie, and positively relishing the occasional visit from a third-shift succubus.

up *adv.*   In the (figurative) direction of being operational, whence the field engineers' Sisyphean task of "getting it up." *Compare* DOWN. *See also* DOWNTIME; UPTIME.

upgrade *n. & v.trans.* [From *up* + Latin *gradus* "steep incline."] **1** *n.* An expensive counterexample to earlier conjectures about upward compatibility. **2** *n.* A painful crisis which belatedly restores one's faith in the previous system. **3** *v.trans.* To replace (obsolete stability) with something less boring. *See also* CONVERSION; OBSOLESCENCE.

♦ Our 360/50, it pleases us plenty;
We bought it last week to replace the 370!
We traded the VM originally installed,
But a second-hand DAT box is worth bugger-all.

uptime *n.* Some future (unspecified) time when the system will be UP and running. *Compare* DOWNTIME. *See also* CRASH.

urn *n.* A high-class jam jar containing colored balls and the ashes of dead statisticians.

user *n.* [Origin: perhaps ironical use of agent noun *user* "one that makes use of," or confusion with *used* "exploited."] **1** *n.* The individual or group invoiced for and waiting to operate certain boxed items lying unopened in another department.

♦Until the items are correctly delivered, decrated, and assembled, the user is also known as a REFERENCE ACCOUNT.

2 *n.* The first of the SEVEN CATASTROPHES OF COMPUTING.

UTM *n.* [Universal Turing Machine.] The top-of-the-range TURING MACHINE, able to simulate any past, present, or future computing system.

♦Theoretically, it can do this using just one BISTABLE element (C. Shannon, 1966) and a lot of tape. The speed of the UTM is limited only by the user's imagination and is not constrained by the trying tardiness of physical elements, such as electrons, which screws the competition. This freedom more than compensates for the archaic, 1930s architecture and the need to write your own ADD subroutine.

VDU *n.* *pronounced* toooob\ [Visual Display Unit.] *See also* CURSOR; GLASS TTY.

verification *n.* An optional method of compounding the errors of data entry: e.g., the situation where Jo(e) decides that the "8" that Fred(a) thought was a "3" is really a "5."

version *n.* *Software* Any one of a series of conflicting, mutilated copies of a lost original.

▶Versions are distinguished, one from the other, by assigning arbitrary tags such as *current, authorized, my, your,* and *latest.* Further subcategorization calls for a variety of local "Dewey-it-yourself" classifications, or an entry in the date-stolen field.

version, latest *n.* That VERSION which most exceeds the DEADLINE for completion.

virtual *adj.* Being or pertaining to a tangible, nonexistent object. "I can see it, but it's not there."—Lady Macbeth. *Compare* TRANSPARENT.

▶Announcing Virtuality a few days before IBM but 7 years after Ferranti, a spokesperson for Irish Business Machines said, "Oh, so it's person, is it, indeed? I'll be having none of that, I tell yer. It's me, Sean, as well you know. Come outside and say that, if you're man enough. . . ." Later, when the presentation had been restructured, the following statement was issued: "Virtual products offer a revolutionary challenge, not only to this company and its customers, but to the entire accounting profession. We are now able to bill well in advance of delivery, deliver well in advance of production, and spend the money long before we invoice. On the other hand, our users can claim tax investment credits and depreciation well in advance of taking delivery. We suggest a new difference-of-the-digits depreciation metolo . . . melthodogoly . . ." (prolonged cheers, waving of order papers, chants of "We want Sean!," counterchants of "Over my dead system!"). The rest is history. . . .

VMOS *n.* [Acronym for Virtual Memory Operating System.] *See* PAGING.

Voltaire-Candide, law of "All is for the best in the best of all possible environments." (originally: "Tout est pour le mieux dans le meilleur des mondes possibles."—*Candide,* Voltaire.)

◆A cynical 18th-century acceptance of the status quo adopted by computer users in the 20th century, but not without some envy of the relatively trouble-free adventures enjoyed by Candide and Pangloss. Among the many familiar observations supporting the law, we offer:

"God sent us this 360, and Lo! our 1400 payroll programs run no slower than before."

"The six-month delivery setback will allow us to refine our flowcharts and build a computer room."

"The file I have just accidentally erased was due for purging sooner or later."

"The more data I punch in this card, the lighter it becomes, and the lower the mailing cost."

"Our system has broken down. We can all retire to the canteen, where the on-site engineer is watching the Big Fight on TV."

"This flowchart, although rejected in toto by the DPM, will nicely cover the crack in the wall above my desk."

"The system has crashed just as I was beginning to suspect an endless loop situation."

"We were freezing during the power outage, until the standby generator caught fire."

VTSO *n.* [Virtual TimeSharing Option (© Irish Business Machines).] An option which allows one teleprinter to support up to 64 × 370/168s (no modem is needed if all units are within a radius of 60 feet).

◆Theoretically a total of 128 × 370/168s can be attached, but response time degrades to an unacceptable level owing to mainframe THRASHING. Also, it becomes physically difficult to meet the 60-foot limit, so the extra cost of modems must be considered. See the accompanying illustration.

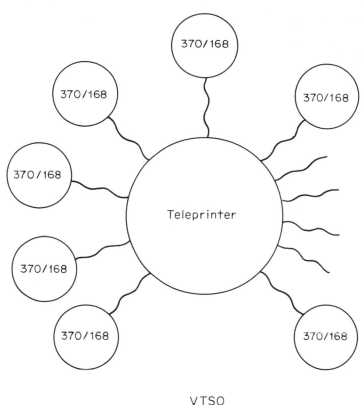

VTSO

VUE *n.*　A text editor available on the Alpha Micro system, the most memorable feature of which is that (Control + L) moves the cursor to the right.

vulnerability *n.*　A measure of the adverse impact which the output of a program or package has on its recipients. *See* PAYROLL.

watergate *n.* A fluid logic switching device.

wheel *n.* A device with so many conflicting applications that each user must reinvent it to ensure satisfaction.

wild card *n.* **1** A symbol which defaults to anything and is therefore mandatory at moments of doubt. *See* DEFAULT. **2** A tab card randomly inserted upside down in a pack to enliven the action. *See also* LUDDITE.

WOM *n.* [Acronym for Write-Only Memory. ©Irish Business Machines.] An early chip designed to implement the POLISH NOTATION, now superseded by the EWOM.

word processing *n.* Any system equipped with a slow, double-case printer.

worst-case design *n.* The one delivered.

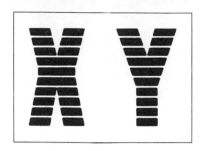

XDS *n.* [Xerox Data Systems.] Abbreviation in use until 1976, when Xerox Corporation decided to concentrate on the traditional, more reliable aspects of reprography.

▶XDS is now used as an abbreviation for eXoDuS, a warning that mortality in the DP arena is not confined to the midgets.

YODALS *n.* [Acronym for Yangtse Opium Den Accounts Leceivable System.] *See* CHINESE TOTAL.

your program *n.* A maze of non sequiturs littered with clever-clever tricks and irrelevant comments. *Compare* MY PROGRAM.